biTe
of Seattle
cookbook vol. IV

Printed in the United States of America
Published by I.P.I. Publishing
10245 Main Street, Suite 8-3
Bellevue, Washington 98004
(206) 454-8473

ISBN 0-939449-04-8

For additional copies write to
I.P.I. Publishing
or use order forms provided
at the back of this book.

▼▼▼▼▼▼▼▼▼▼▼▼▼▼▼▼▼▼▼▼▼▼▼▼▼▼▼▼▼

Judith Deak
Gretchen Flickinger
Publishers

Gretchen Flickinger
Cover Design, Production

Abraxas Typesetting
Typesetting

Overlake Press
Printing

Photos courtesy of Festivals Inc.

Table of Contents

The chefs at the Bite
Invite you to try
Delectable "secrets"
From swordfish to pie.

Dazzle your friends
With an eggroll or two
Cappelletti with meat sauce
Or hearty beef stew.

The Best of the Bite's
In this great, little book
So just turn the page
And get ready to cook.

P.O. Box 131
Long Beach, Washington 98631

Anna Lena's Cranberry Products are made from Washington grown cranberries and other high quality ingredients. They are made with the care and tradition of fine cooking passed down from my maternal great-grandmother, Anna Lena Berg. I hope you enjoy using and cooking with this and other Anna Lena's Cranberry Products as much as I have enjoyed bringing them to you.

—*Karen Snyder*

Gordon's Gearhart Chicken

Serves 8

4 chicken breasts
Marinade:
1 10-oz jar Anna Lena's
   Cranberry Port Jelly
½ tsp sage

½ tsp thyme
½ tsp black pepper
1 Tbsp Anna Lena's Sweet,
   Hot Cranberry Mustard

Bone, skin and split chicken breasts.

Combine Port Jelly, spices and mustard. Marinate chicken two hours or overnight.

Arrange chicken breasts in ovenproof dish. Pour marinade over the top. Bake 35 – 45 minutes at 350°, basting occasionally.

Long Beach Sunrise

Serves 8

1 Tbsp unsalted butter
4 Golden Delicious apples
¼ c. water

1 10-oz jar Anna Lena's
  Cranberry Citrus Marmalade
8 sprigs fresh mint

Lightly butter microwave-proof dish.

Cut apples horizontally and core. Arrange in baking dish, cut side up. Add water to pan. Spoon 2 Tbsp marmalade into each cavity.

Microwave on high 8–12 minutes until apples are soft and marmalade bubbly.

Let stand 10 minutes. Garnish with fresh mint.

Cranberry Chicken Crepes

▼▼

Serves 6

12 crepes
4 chicken breast halves
2 Tbsp butter
⅓ cup onion, minced
1 clove garlic, minced

½ cup chicken broth
¼ cup Anna Lena's Spiced
    Cranberry vinegar
¾ cup sour cream

Skin and bone chicken breasts. Slice chicken into thin strips. Saute in butter until opaque. Remove from pan.

Saute onions and garlic. When translucent, add chicken stock. Simmer 10 minutes.

Add spiced cranberry vinegar. Cook on high until stock is reduced to ⅓ cup.

Stir in sour cream. Simmer 1 minute and stir in chicken strips.

Remove chicken strips. Arrange on crepes. Roll up and place in oven-proof dish. Pour sauce over top. Bake at 350° for 20 minutes.

*Make your favorite crepe recipe or use purchased prepared crepes.

Bahn Thai

409 Roy Street
Seattle, Washington 98109
(206) 283-0444

Bahn Thai Restaurant has been chosen as Best Thai Restaurant within the Puget Sound area in three consecutive years: 1986 Silver Spoon Award from Northwest Gourmet; 1987 The Best of Seattle from The Weekly; 1988 Reader Poll awards from Pacific Northwest Magazine.

We very much appreciate all your support and will try our best to continue serving you delicious, authentic Thai cuisine.

Phad Thai Noodle

Serves 3-4

1 lb Thai rice noodles
2 eggs
1 cup bean sprouts
2 Tbsp ground peanuts
1 Tbsp sugar
1 Tbsp fish sauce

1 Tbsp white vinegar
1 tsp minced garlic
1 Tbsp dry tofu*
½ cup vegetable oil
1 Tbsp salted turnip*

If using fresh noodles, skip this paragraph. If using dry noodles, soak them in warm water for 15 minutes. Drain. In a frying pan put all the oil. Brown the garlic until light brown. Add eggs, breaking the yolk, then add noodles and fry. Add sugar, fish sauce, vinegar, tofu, ground peanuts and bean sprouts.

Fresh noodles: heat oil in frying pan. Add garlic and cook till lightly brown. Add eggs, breaking yolks. Add noodles and fry two to three minutes. Add remaining ingredients. Heat through and serve.

* Salted turnip: salted and dried Daikon radish used as a seasoning in stir-fried dishes, soups and stuffed buns. Salted turnip and tofu are both available in Asian markets.

Biringer Farm

4625 – 40th Pl NE
Marysville, Washington 98270
(206) 259-0255

Biringer Strawberries has been in Marysville for over 40 years. That's three generations of Biringer Farmers producing the best strawberries in the Northwest.

Biringer Farm is located on an island in the delta of the Snohomish River. In the past harvests were shipped by barge, instead of freighted by wagon.

At Biringer Farm you can get your berries almost any way you want them. Can't pick your own? That's okay, we have them fresh picked by the flat. No time to clean and slice? No problem! Try our convenient already washed and sliced berry pack. All you have to do is serve them! For a special treat, try the Biringer Gourmet Jam.

Frozen Strawberry Pie

Serves 6–8

Filling:

1½ cups sliced fresh berries
   (or 10 oz. frozen, thawed)
1 cup sour cream
1 cup sugar
1 egg white

Crust:

1½ cups vanilla wafers
½ cup melted butter
½ cup chopped walnuts
(chocolate wafers can be used
   for other pies)

Filling: Beat the egg white, berries and sugar on high speed for about 8 minutes. When soft peaks appear, gently fold in the sour cream.

Spoon (pile) into the prepared crust. Freeze 15 minutes. Swirl top, put back in freezer.

Crust: Mix wafer crumbs, walnuts, and butter. Press into pie pan. Bake in hot oven about 10 minutes.

Strawberry Bread

▼▼

Makes 1 loaf

Part 1:

1 10-oz package frozen strawberries, thawed and undrained

2 eggs

¾ cup oil

Part 2:

1½ cups all-purpose flour

½ teaspoon baking soda

1 cup sugar

1 tsp cinnamon

Part 1: Whisk eggs and oil in small bowl. Puree strawberries in blender or food processor.

Part 2: Combine dry ingredients in large bowl. Add strawberries and egg-oil mixture and mix well, using a wooden spoon.

Pour into a greased and floured 9x5-inch loaf pan. Bake at 325° for about 70 minutes (or until toothpick inserted in center comes out clean).

Remove bread from pan 5 minutes after removing from oven. Cool loaf completely on wire rack.

Strawberry or Raspberry Shortcake

▼▼

Serves 4

2 cups Bisquick mix
⅔ cup milk
2 Tbsp sugar
1 egg

¼ cup melted butter
1 qt strawberries or raspberries
whipping cream

Beat first five ingredients vigorously 30 seconds. If dough is too sticky, gradually add Bisquick mix (up to ¼ cup) to make easy to handle. Knead 10 times. Roll out on well dusted board ½" thick.

Bake in round ungreased pan 8–10 minutes at 450°.

Split shortcake into two layers. Spoon berries between layers and on top. Top berries with whipping cream. Garnish with whole berries.

500 S. Bonair Road
Zillah, Washington 98953
(509) 829-6027

Eggs Bonair

▼▼

Serves 4

4 eggs

3 oz can of anchovy fillets

½ cup mayonnaise

lettuce leaves

2 Tbsp capers

4 sprigs fresh parsley

Hard boil eggs. Halve lengthwise and lay both halves on a crisp lettuce leaf.

Drain oil from anchovies and mix with mayonnaise. Place a spoonful of mayonnaise on each egg. Carefully lay two fillets of anchovy lengthwise on mayonnaise. Sprinkle capers over the eggs letting the extras fall to the lettuce.

Garnish with parsley.

Serve with Bonair 1987 Chateau Puryear Reserve Chardonnay.

Poached Rockfish au Sauce Puryear

▼▼

Serves 4

4 6-oz Pacific rockfish fillets

1½ cups white sauce

1 cup finely chopped oysters

½ cup finely chopped capers

Rinse rockfish in fresh water. Steam until thickest part of fish flakes.

Just before serving, bring white sauce to near boiling and add the oysters and capers. Place fillet on serving plate and cover with sauce.

Serve with wild rice and a garnish of parsley and a twist of lemon. We recommend serving Bonair Chateau Puryear Chardonnay.

Bonair Winery House Dressing

Makes 3 cups

2 cups olive oil
1 cup dill pickle juice
1 Tbsp red wine vinegar

2 cloves fresh garlic
1 Tbsp Worcestershire sauce
½ tsp salt

Mix olive oil and dill pickle juice in a small mixing bowl and mix with a high-speed hand mixer. Add Tbsp of red wine vinegar.

Peel garlic. Put in a garlic press and press directly into the bowl. Add Worcestershire sauce. Add salt. Mix into a froth. Let stand in the refrigerator one hour before serving.

2125 1st Avenue, Suite #102
Seattle, Washington 98121
(206) 728-1461

Welcome to Brasil! Welcome to the only Brasilian food experience west of the Mississippi and north of San Francisco. With
Brasil restaurant, you can explore the delicacies, colorful dishes,
and flavorful cuisine of this magical and mysterious country.

"Brasilians love to eat and Brasil restaurant showed me why."
—Wanda Adams, *P.I.* critic. "Delicious... charming... exceptional."
—*Gourmet Notebook.*

Introducing Seattle to the Brasilian culture from its Belltown
location at 1st & Blanchard, Brasil Restaurant offers something
new for the simple or sophisticated appetite. Feijoada, the national
dish of Brasil, is a multi-cultural feast! This Portuguese, West
African and native Brasilian Indian dish is commonly prepared to
receive family and friends or to commemorate any important event.
It is a fun array of meats, sausages, bacon smoked meats served
with a delicious black bean sauce, vegetable vinaigrette, farofa,
rice, and collard greens.

"Bom apetite" and "boa viagem."

Feijoada Completa

▼▼▼

Serves 15

5 cups black beans
1 lb jerked beef
1 sm smoked tongue
½ lb Canadian bacon
1 lb fresh pork sausages
1 lb corned spareribs
1 lb smoked sausages (kielbasa)
1 lb Portuguese sausages
½ lb lean bacon
1 lb lean beef, cut in cubes
1 Tbsp shortening

3 lg chopped onions
5 crushed garlic cloves
2 chopped bell peppers
1 Tbsp chopped parsley
1 can (med) tomato sauce
salt and black pepper to taste
beef and chicken stock
malagueta peppers* (from Brazil, or Tabasco pepper, optional)
bay leaves
1 grilled pork chop per guest

Wash beans well, drain and add 4 cups of water, 2 cups of beef stock, and 1 cup of chicken stock. Bring just to boiling, cover, and reduce to a simmer. At this stage, add a handful of bay leaves, the jerked beef and lean beef in cubes and the spareribs. Cook smoked tongue separately for 10 minutes in a little water, then peel and add to the beans.

As soon as beans are cooking, add the chopped onions, bell peppers, malagueta or tabasco, parsley and 3 Tbsp of sodium bicarbonate (dissolved in water first). It helps to cook the beans and turns this dish more digestive and light. Add water and beef stock as needed till beans are tender.

Note: this dish takes 2½ hours to prepare and all the meats should be added within the first hour.

While the beans are cooking, cut the Canadian bacon and the lean bacon in cubes and fry till light golden brown. Put aside and use the leftover fat to fry all the sausages. Add this combination after 2 hours.

When beans are tender and all the meat and sausages have been added, add the tomato sauce. Stir well and let cook for 10 minutes. In a saucepan, saute garlic with shortening and butter and add to the pot. Mix well, adjust the seasoning and enjoy your feijoada.

Serve with rice, thin sliced collard greens sauteed with butter and crushed garlic, a grilled pork chop, sweetened orange slices (optional) and farofa.

Farofa: fry three eggs in bacon fat or butter, mix with sliced onions, garlic, parsley, green olives and sliced sausages. When golden brown, mix with manioc meal* or 2 cups of bread crumbs. It is served as a side dish.

* Manioc meal (farinha de mandioca) and malagueta peppers can be found in El Mercado Latino at the Pike Place Market.

10733 Northup Way at 108th Ave.
Bellevue, Washington 98008
(206) 827-8585

Bravo, acclaimed as one of the very best in the Northwest, serves exceptional Italian food in the ambience of an Italian villa. The open kitchen in the center fulfills the menu's promise of excellence, from traditional Italian dishes to novel adaptations using first-quality fresh seafood, aged beef, local milk-fed veal, fresh pasta, fresh herbs and imported cheeses. The wood-fired oven and gourmet pizzas add just the right touch of informality. Those of Italian descent can have their name and village painted on Bravo's famous heritage map. Open daily for lunch, 11:30 a.m. to 2:00 p.m. Dinner, 5:30 to 10:00 p.m.; except Friday and Saturday, until 11:00 p.m. Sunday, dinner only, 4:30 to 9:30 p.m. AE, MC, V.

Tiramisu - "Pick Me Up"

Serves 6–8

2 eggs, separated
3 Tbsp sugar
9 oz Marscapone
(soft Italian cream cheese)
4 shots espresso
(instant may be substituted)

2 oz sweet Marsala
3 Tbsp sugar
3 packages ladyfingers
3 oz shaved chocolate

Brew espresso, add sugar and Marsala. Mix well to dissolve sugar.

Whip egg whites until stiff, set aside.

Whip egg yolks with 3 Tbsp sugar until light in color, add marscapone and mix well. Fold in egg whites.

Line bread pan with parchment. Line bottom and sides with ladyfingers, brush with espresso mixture to lightly saturate. Spread marscapone mixture over the ladyfingers (approximately ¼" thick). Sprinkle with shaved chocolate. Alternate ladyfingers, marscapone mixture and chocolate, ending with ladyfingers. Refrigerate until firm (at least 4 hours).

Remove from pan and frost top and sides with marscapone mixture and sprinkle with shaved chocolate. Slice and garnish with chocolate.

Bravo's Agnalotti di Branchio (Crab Filled Pasta)

▼▼▼

Serves 4

Cheese pasta filling:
¾ cup cream cheese
2 cups ricotta
¼ cup parmesan cheese
1 egg
¼ bunch spinach, lightly sauteed
  in olive oil and drained well
⅛ tsp salt
⅛ tsp pepper

Crab sauce:
6 cups whipping cream
2 Tbsp butter, softened
¼ Tbsp lemon juice
½ tsp fresh marjoram
1 cup Dungeness crab meat,
  drained well

You may purchase a mild cheese filled agnalotti* or ravioli or prepare your own using this recipe.

Prepare a basic fresh pasta recipe and fill with the cheese pasta filling. For the filling, combine all filling ingredients in a food processor and mix until well blended.

For the crab sauce, combine whipping cream and butter and cook over medium-high heat until reduced by half. Add lemon juice and marjoram. Remove from heat and stir in crab meat.

Drop pasta into lightly salted boiling water and cook until *al dente*. Drain pasta and mix with crab sauce. Garnish with a fresh marjoram sprig.

* Agnalotti: Crescent shaped filled pasta (dumpling).

Agnello Bravo (Lamb Bravo)

▼▼

Serves 6–8

Lamb roast:
4-5 lb lamb roast
1 tsp salt
1 tsp black pepper
3 Tbsp olive oil
Carmelized onions:
2 cups sliced white onions
4 Tbsp olive oil

Artichoke mousse:
1½ cups canned artichoke hearts
  (not marinated)
⅛ cup heavy cream
¼ cup unsalted butter, softened
½ tsp fresh lemon juice
⅛ tsp salt
⅛ tsp white pepper

Carmelized onions and artichoke mousse can be prepared while meat cooks or a day in advance.

For onions: heat olive oil over high heat in saute pan. Add onions and reduce heat to medium low. Cook for 30–45 minutes until onions are a dark caramel color. Stir often.

For artichoke mousse: drain artichokes and remove tough outer leaves. Puree in food processor with cream until smooth. With motor running, slowly add lemon juice, softened butter, salt and pepper. Blend well. Just prior to serving, warm slowly in a double boiler. Do not overheat or mousse will separate.

For roast: while oven heats to 375°, sear seasoned roast in olive oil until brown on all sides. Place on roasting pan and bake for approximately 20–25 minutes per pound, or until meat thermometer reaches 125–130°. Baste occasionally with the oil. Remove roast from oven. Let rest for 15 minutes, then slice. Arrange carmelized onions on a plate, then slices of lamb and top with the warm artichoke mousse.

5701 6th Avenue South
Seattle, Washington
(206) 763-2215

300 120th Avenue Northeast
Bellevue, Washington
(206) 455-3930

An upscale steakhouse featuring prime rib, aged steaks, barbecued and baby-back ribs, and fresh fish specialties. Glass enclosed greenhouse dining is available off the main dining room in Bellevue. Seattle features a Sports Bar with four TV monitors.

Barbecue Baby Back Pork Ribs

Makes 1 full rack

pork ribs, 1¼ to 1½ slab
liquid smoke (Wrights)
2 cups water
BBQ sauce
chopped parsley

Seasoning salt:
½ cup salt
1 Tbsp ground black pepper
1 tsp celery salt
1 Tbsp onion powder
1 Tbsp garlic powder

Brush both sides of slab with Wrights liquid smoke. Rub seasoning salt on top side lightly.

Place bow side up in 2" high sided pan with 2 cups of water. Cover and bake for 1¾ hours at 275°. Remove from oven and chill.

When ready to serve, baste both sides with BBQ sauce and place on broiler rack. Charbroil 5 minutes each side, or until hot.

Remove from oven and baste top with BBQ sauce.

With knife cut ¾ of the way through the rib next to the bone. Sprinkle with chopped parsley.

305 Harrison #201
Seattle, Washington 98109

Located in the Seattle Center House, Cafe Europe is in one of Seattle's richest cultural and artistic entertainment oriented areas. Cafe Europe is modeled after a European sidewalk cafe. It is open seven days a week for breakfast, lunch and dinner. The menu features Italian specialty items, gourmet burgers and sandwiches. Cafe Europe also offers authentic Italian roasted espresso coffees, full cocktail service as well as a variety of imported and domestic beers.

Whether you're interested in a European style dining experience, or simply want to relax with a cappucino, brandy or chocolate mousse cake, Cafe Europe provides a unique, cheerful environment and delicious food and beverages.

25

Chicken & Artichoke Hearts
in Light Lemon Sauce

▼▼▼

Serves 4

4 8-oz flattened, boneless,
  skinless chicken breasts
32 artichoke hearts, quartered
8 Tbsp butter
2 Tbsp olive oil

4 cloves garlic, minced
¼ cup fresh lemon juice
fresh minced parsley
salt & pepper to taste

Saute chicken breast over medium high heat in 4 Tbsp butter and olive oil until opaque. Remove from pan and set aside. Season with salt and pepper

Saute garlic in pan drippings and remaining butter until translucent.

Add artichoke hearts and saute over high heat until heated through.

Add lemon juice and allow mixture to boil for 30 seconds. Pour over chicken breasts, sprinkle with minced parsley and garnish with fresh lemon slices.

Cafe Europe Cooler

▼▼

Serves 4

2 cups white wine
½ cup fresh squeezed orange juice
¼ cup fresh squeezed lemon juice

¼ cup fresh squeezed lime juice
2 cups gingerale
ice

Blend all ingredients and pour into pint glasses that have been filled with ice.

Garnish with lemon twists and orange slices.

Almond Baked Brie in Puff Pastry

▼▼

Makes 24–48 servings

1 6-lb wheel of French Brie *3 12"-square sheets puff pastry**

2 cups chopped almonds *1 egg*

2 Tbsp butter *water*

Preheat oven to 425°.

In a large heavy skillet, toast almonds until golden brown over high heat. Brush top of brie with melted butter. Sprinkle with toasted almonds and press lightly to imbed almonds.

Roll two puff pastry sheets until ⅛" thick; slightly larger in diameter than cheese. Place Brie wheel on top of 1 sheet, cover with the other. Pinch sides together and trim off extra dough. Beat 1 egg with 2 tsp of water, and brush over top and sides of Brie, reserving some mixture.

Cut out leaves, flowers or other desired shapes from remaining sheet of dough. Place design on top of wheel. Avoid more than 2 layers of puff pastry. Score leaves with knife for more detail.

Brush remaining surfaces with rest of egg mixture. Bake for ½ hour or until golden brown.

* Available in the frozen food section of most supermarkets.

CAFELOC

407 Broad Street
Seattle, Washington 98109
(206) 441-6883

Seattle Center House
Seattle, Washington 98109
(206) 728-9292

Cafe Loc was established in January 1978 in a small building located at the corner of John and Broad in downtown Seattle by a former Saigon lawyer and an army officer who arrived as a refugee couple from Vietnam.

It is a specialty restaurant serving Vietnamese and oriental vegetarian dishes. Cafe Loc has been well received by the eating public, because of reasonable prices, excellent foods, and, above all, personal family-style service.

Cafe Loc has been consistently praised by the Seattle press as "the best Vietnamese food in town." In 1988 the Seattle Weekly awarded "Best Eggroll" to Cafe Loc.

Cha Goo (Vietnamese Spring Roll)

▼▼▼

Makes 2 dozen

1 lb ground pork or
  1 cup of minced tofu

1 oz black fungus, minced*

1 sm package of bean thread
  cut into small pieces

1 med onion, minced

2 carrots, grated

½ tsp salt

½ tsp black pepper

1 tsp sugar

½ tsp garlic powder

1 lb bean sprouts

24 egg roll wrappers

rice paper or lumpia

Mix ground pork or tofu with all the vegetables. Season with salt, pepper, sugar and garlic powder.

Wrap 1 heaping Tbsp of mixture in each wrapper and deep fry till golden brown.

Serve hot with fresh lettuce, cucumber, bean sprouts and fish sauce.

Wrap egg roll in lettuce along with other vegetables and dip in fish sauce.

* Available in dried form at Asian markets.

FRESH
MADE

ICE
CREAMS

4519 University Way NE
Seattle, Washington 98105
(206) 545-7147

C'est Moo is a warm and friendly place right on the "Ave" in the center of the University District.

C'est Moo is proud to be the producer of one of the finest premium ice creams in the Seattle area. The ice cream is made from a mix prepared specially in an enriched form with no preservatives or stabilizers used. Only the finest ingredients imported from many places in the world are used. The chocolate is the very best in solid form which is melted and then folded into the mix. Fresh fruit is used when in season. Artificial flavoring or coloring is never used in any C'est Moo Ice Cream.

At C'est Moo there are many varieties of mix-ins to enhance the flavor of the ice cream, while the mix-in process tempers the ice cream for greater enjoyment. Finally, your delicious selection is placed in a freshly made waffle cone for you to enjoy.

C'est Moo Mud Pie

▼▼

Serves 8

9" chocolate crumb pie shell

18 oz peanut butterfinger
  ice cream

27 oz real chocolate ice cream

4 oz peanut butter

4 oz fudge topping

4 oz granulated peanuts

3 oz chocolate ice cream shell
  topping

7" diameter x 2½" deep stainless
  bowl

Fill pie shell with C'est Moo Peanut Butterfinger ice cream. Fill stainless bowl with C'est Moo Real Chocolate ice cream. Place both in freezer until hard. Heat peanut butter, fudge topping, and shell topping until liquid. Sprinkle 3 oz of peanuts on pie shell base. Cover with melted peanut butter and fudge topping.

Remove Real Chocolate ice cream from mold by dipping mold in warm water for approximately 5 seconds to loosen. Place ice cream mold upside down on prepared pie shell base. Ladle shell topping over top so it runs down the sides. Sprinkle remainder of peanuts on top. Place in freezer.

Use a knife dipped in warm water to cut and serve. Pie is best cut at between 0° and 5°. Smother each slice in whipped cream, top with a cherry and enjoy!

THE
CONTINENTAL PASTRY SHOP

4549 University Way NE
Seattle, Washington 98105
(206) 632-4700

A Seattle institution since 1967, The Continental, as it is affectionately known, has been a family-owned operation that prides itself on superior, village-inspired, Greek cuisine.

Besides being a well-known restaurant, it is also a "Bakaliko" (Greek deli), cafe, intellectual meeting ground, and pastry shop that serves superb Copenhagen, traditional walnut baklava, revani and kataifi.

We specialize in our own handmade "Loukanico" (Greek sausage) made on the premises, along with "Spanakopita" (fresh spinach pie), "Kotopoulo" (chicken with spices) and will next introduce traditional country recipes for lamb, fish and other dishes.

The Lagos family is there to greet you and provide good cheer. This family feeling transcends all we do and inspires us to continue many more years of fine Greek cuisine.

33

Spanakopita (Spinach & Feta Cheese Pie)

▼▼

Serves 8–10

5 bunches spinach	½ lb fillo (dough)*
2 bunches green onions	1 cup olive oil
¾ lb feta cheese	fresh dill
8 oz cottage cheese (small curd)	fresh mint leaves
6 eggs	pinch of black pepper

Clean and finely chop spinach and green onions. Mix spinach, onions, mint leaves, dill, pepper, and oil together in large bowl. Grease 12" x 17" pan with olive oil. Beat eggs and mix in another bowl with crumbled feta and cottage cheese. Mix egg and cheese mixture into spinach mixture.

Place 4 fillo leaves in bottom of pan. Divide the remaining fillo in approximately 4 equal quantities. Place each set of leaves two inches into the pan leaving most of the leaves hanging outside of the pan on the table. Place the filling evenly throughout the pan.

Fold the overhanging fillo on top of the filling and oil. Bake in 350° oven until brown (approximately ½ hour).

* Fillo/Phylo dough is available at Greek markets and specialty delicatessens in Seattle, i.e., at De Laurenti's in the Pike Place Market.

Queen Anne
236 1st Ave West
Seattle, Washington
(206) 283-4400

Bellevue
10116 NE 8th
Bellevue, Washington
(206) 455-5775

Lake Union
901 Fairview Ave N
Seattle, Washington
(206) 382-9963

Need a change of pace? Try Duke's – not just another bar and grill. Fresh seafood, #1 clam chowder, tasty drinks, homemade desserts, great cheeseburgers and wonderful people. What more could you ask for? Queen Anne, Bellevue and Lake Union is where you'll find us. Do yourself a favor. Go to Duke's. It's good for you.

Duke's #1 Clam Chowder

▼▼

Makes one quart (6–8 servings)

3 oz diced bacon (approx 4 slices)

1 medium diced onion

3 stalks diced celery

¼ lb diced new potatoes (blanched)

4 cups heavy cream

1½ cups chopped clams, fresh or frozen

⅓ cup flour

½ cup half & half

3 oz butter

2 oz clam concentrate or clam base

1¼ cups clam juice or nectar

1 pinch chopped fresh garlic, white pepper, black pepper, cayenne pepper to taste

1 tsp marjoram

2 tsp chopped fresh basil

1 tsp Italian seasoning

¼ tsp dill

½ tsp thyme

2 bay leaves

⅛ cup chopped fresh parsley

Cook bacon until transparent. Add butter, onions, celery and all the seasoning except dill and parsley. Cook until tender. Add flour and cook for 3–4 minutes over low heat. Add all dairy products, clam nectar and base. Heat just under boiling point. Steam potatoes and cool. Add chopped clams and potatoes. Bring to a boil slowly and cook for 2–3 minutes. Add dill and parsley and serve. Enjoy!

Duke's Chocolate Chip Cookies

Approximately 15 larges cookies

1 lb fresh butter
1½ cups light brown sugar
1½ cups granulated sugar
2 tsp pure vanilla
4 medium eggs

2 tsp salt
1 Tbsp baking soda
4½ cups flour
3½ cups chocolate chips
3½ cups walnuts (broken)

Cream together butter and sugars, scraping sides of bowl. Add vanilla. Slowly add eggs, incorporating fully.

Combine dry ingredients and add ⅛ at a time until completely mixed. On high speed add walnuts. On slow speed add chocolate chips. Drop by tablespoons onto baking sheets.

Bake in 350° oven for 12 – 15 minutes until golden brown.

15600 NE 8th Street
Bellevue, Washington 98008
(206) 641-4352

About our name: EBRU is a traditional Turkish art. Little is known about the origins of the art of EBRU or marbling. The oldest known example of EBRU, whose practitioners today are precious and few, dates to 1554.

The term itself comes from the Persian word meaning eyebrow and cloud. One type of EBRU is known as "battal" (or plain). EBRU consists of forms reminiscent of eyebrow and cloud shapes. The materials used in making EBRU are dye (all earthern), kitre (gum tragacanth), od (bile), tekre (trough), firca (brush), combs, wire, paper (almost any kind) and muhre (polishing stone).

EBRU in light colors is used as a background for calligraphy, bookbinding and other forms of art.

In the Mediterranean, names give meaning to the establishment in which they are named. We believe our service and food are quality – just as the Turkish art of EBRU.

We are open 7 days a week for lunch, dinner, and take home. We offer personalized off-premises catering. Come and enjoy our 5 different kinds of baklava, fresh juice bar, hot gyro sandwiches, many mouthwatering Mediterranean salads and grocery items.

39

Hunkar Begendi (Sultan's Delight)

▼▼

Serves 6–8

4 lbs eggplant

2 lbs lamb meat, cut in small
   pieces

2 cups milk

¾ cup flour

½ cup butter

½ cup cheese (Kashar or Gruyere)

2 lg tomatoes, peeled, seeded, and
   chopped

2 med onions, chopped

salt, pepper, bay leaf

This dish is composed of meat surrounded by eggplant puree. To prepare the meat: in a large skillet over medium heat, brown the meat and add onions, tomatoes, salt, pepper, and a bay leaf. Do not add water. Cover and simmer for 1½ hours.

To prepare the eggplant: cook the eggplant by holding it by the stem and turning it over an open flame (gas).* When the eggplant is soft, remove it from the flame. When it has cooled, remove the skin with a knife. Mash with a fork in large bowl and set aside.

Melt half the butter in a saucepan. Add the flour to make a paste. Add the milk slowly and bring to a boil. Add the eggplant puree to this sauce and stir for 6 to 7 minutes on low heat. Finally, add the grated cheese and stir. Put the meat in the center of the serving platter and surround with the puree.

*Eggplant can also be placed under a broiler, turning frequently, until the skin blisters and eggplant is soft.

Pirincli Pilic (Chicken with Rice)

▼▼

Serves 4

1 2-lb chicken (reserve liver)
2 cups rice
3 Tbsp butter
3 Tbsp pine nuts
3 Tbsp currants
1 bunch dill

1 finely chopped onion
½ tsp salt
1 peeled, finely chopped tomato
1 chicken liver, diced
4 cups meat broth

Soak rice ½ hour in warm water, then drain. Do the same with the currants. Wash pine nuts.

Melt 1 Tbsp butter in a saucepan and brown the chicken on all sides. Add the onions and brown. Add liver, tomato, currants, salt and broth. Boil for 10 minutes.

In another pan melt the remaining butter and brown the rice and pine nuts. Transfer rice mixture to the saucepan containing the chicken. Cover and cook over low heat for 20 minutes.

Garnish with parsley and additional browned pine nuts.

ELLIOTT'S

ON THE PIER

PIER 56   623-4340

Pier 56
Seattle, Washington 98101
(206) 623-4340

Seattleites savor fine seafood and appreciate a great view. We all take pride in telling friends and guests of our latest catch, the best view of Puget Sound, and the best place to combine them both for an excellent dining experience. And where do so many Seattleites tell their friends and visitors to go to view the best as they eat the best? Elliott's on the Pier – of course!

Elliott's combines everything that is great about Seattle with everything wonderful about a dining experience. Located at the end of Pier 56 in the Trident building, Elliott's features a panoramic view of Puget Sound. In a setting of warm teak wood, greenhouse windows, comfortable tables and booths, and an open view kitchen, Elliott's prepares the best seafood the Northwest has to offer.

Over a broiler of mesquite charcoal, our chefs prepare a variety of items from salmon to halibut to swordfish. Nothing is ordinary and everything is impeccable. Add fresh pastas, large delicious salads, home-made soups, crab cakes, and a great selection of appetizers, and you have a menu that appeals to novices and dining gourmets alike.

Known for its house-made Sicilian bread (which is complimentary with every entree), its large outdoor dining area, its friendly service and its landmark location, Elliott's on the Pier is indeed a unique experience in a land of plenty.

43

Oysters Elliott

▼▼

Serves 6

30 oysters, shucked on the ½ shell
½ qt mayonnaise
1 cup chili sauce
3 oz horseradish
1 Tbsp lemon juice
1½ tsp Dijon mustard

1½ cups sourdough bread crumbs
½ tsp paprika
1 Tbsp garlic
pinch salt
black pepper
rock salt (for baking)

Shuck and cut oyster abductor muscle, freeing oyster from shell. Keep oyster in shell and arrange oysters over a layer of rock salt on a baking sheet.

Combine all ingredients in a mixing bowl, adding bread crumbs last. Place about a Tbsp of mixture over each oyster.

Bake in a pre-heated oven at 350° till topping turns golden brown (not burning!)

Serve with dry Riesling, Sauvignon Blanc, or Semillon wine.

Golden Banner

458 Hardie Ave SW
Renton, Washington 98055
(206) 255-4546

Mongolian Beef

VVVVVVVVVVVVVVVVVVVVVVVVVVVVVVVVVVVVVVVVVVVVVVVVVVVVVVVVVVVVVV

Serves 2

1 lb lean beef	½ green pepper
4 tsp wine	2½ Tbsp vegetable oil
3 tsp soy sauce	1 tsp Chinese dry blackbean
¼ tsp salt	1 tsp cornstarch
⅓ tsp sugar	1 tsp oyster sauce
⅓ tsp garlic powder	1 tsp sugar
dash of monosodium glutamate	dash of black pepper
dash of black pepper	2 Tbsp water
½ onion	

Slice the beef into 2"x1" thin strips. Shred onion and green pepper.

Put the beef in a bowl, add the wine and mix well. Then add the next six ingredients to season.

Heat 1 Tbsp of oil in a large skillet and throw in the shredded green pepper and onion. Stir-fry for 3–4 minutes. Remove from pan.

Add 2 Tbsp oil to the oil remaining in the skillet and heat. Add the beef; stir-fry quickly. Fry the beef until it changes color. Remove from skillet.

Add ½ Tbsp of oil to the skillet, stir-fry the Chinese black bean for 10 seconds. Add oyster sauce, sugar, pepper and 1 Tbsp water.

Combine cornstarch and 1 Tbsp water and stir into pan. Add beef and vegetables, toss to coat with sauce and heat through. Serve immediately.

*Dry black bean/fermented black beans: black beans that have been preserved in a salty brine and then dried. Available in Asian markets and Uwajimaya.

GRAVITY BAR

86 Pine Street
Seattle, Washington 98101
(206) 443-9694

415 Broadway East
Seattle, Washington 98102
(206) 325-7186

The Gravity Bar was established in June 1986 at Pike Place. Our menu is both inventive and unique, for it reflects our background in mixed, natural foods from macrobiotics to raw foods. From Chef Asa Bron of Visions Unlimited we learned to prepare fresh seafood and vegetarian style dishes.

Coincidentally, The Gravity Bar opened on the 300th birthday of Newton's discovery of gravity.

Breakfast, lunch and dinner are served all day.

Spicy Noodle Salad

▼▼▼

Serves 4–6

1 pkg 8-10 oz soba noodles*
  (40% buckwheat)*
¼ cup dry hiziki seaweed*
¼ cup shoyu
¼ cup sesame oil, toasted
2 Tbsp sesame seeds
¼ cup chopped green onions

2 tsp hot red pepper flakes
½ cup thinly sliced red bell
  peppers
½ cup broccoli flowerettes
½ cup cauliflowerettes
½ cup matchstick carrots

Cook soba noodles for 4 minutes or until done *al dente.*

Soak hiziki in 2 cups water for 20 minutes, then simmer for 10 minutes on low heat, rinse and drain well.

Toss soba in bowl with shoyu, sesame oil, sesame seeds, green onions and both red peppers.

Lightly steam broccoli, cauliflower and carrots for a minute or two, or blanche 1 minute. Add to noodles and toss. Chill and serve.

* Buckwheat soba noodles, toasted sesame oil and hiziki seaweed are available from co-ops, health food stores, and Uwajimaya.

I-Tal Stew (from Jamaica)

▼▼▼

Serves 8–10

1 fresh coconut
1 large onion
1 potato
1 sweet potato
2 zucchini
1 stalk broccoli
1 small cauliflower
okra (optional)

2 carrots
2 stalks celery
4 ears corn, broken into 3 pieces
    each cob
any other vegetables if desired
Garnish:
slivered green onions
diced red or yellow peppers

Split the coconut, dig out the white meat from shell (throw away the milk, if fermented at all). Using a champion juicer, with homogenizer blank instead of screen, run the white meat through the juicer. It will resemble an oily pulp. Wrap the coconut pulp in cheesecloth, forming a bag, or put in a fine strainer. Over a large bowl pour about 2 qts boiling water through the coconut to extract the oils and flavors. Reserve liquid. Squeeze water out of coconut.

Meanwhile, chop all of the vegetables up into hearty chunk-like pieces (except for green onions and peppers used for garnish). Bring reserved liquid to a boil in a large pot. Starting with onions and potatoes, add to coconut stock and resume boiling; add remaining vegetables. Reduce heat and cook for two hours.

If more liquid is needed, repeat pouring boiling water through coconut pulp, and add as needed. Season with a little salt, thyme and black pepper. Spice it up with a dash of cayenne, if desired.

Add corn-on-the-cob pieces 20 minutes before serving; they will float in the stew. Pick out of soup to eat (very ethnic and fun!). Garnish with green onions and diced peppers.

49

CAFFÈ ITALIANO

Ristorante & Catering
2301 N 30th
Tacoma, Washington 98403
(206) 627-0231

Cafe
16943 Southcenter Parkway
Tukwila, Washington 98188
(206) 575-1606

Overlooking the bay in Tacoma, Grazie features the finest in Northern Italian cuisine presented in a warm, elegant atmosphere. Menu selections include antipasto, espresso and desserts prepared in our fully stocked Italian deli, or try our fresh pastas, seafood and veal selections. Lunch, Monday through Friday; dinner, nightly. Outdoor seating and lounge.

Grazie cafe conveniently located three blocks south of Southcenter Mall features our antipasti, espresso, poultry, pastas and desserts. Come watch our cooks prepare your meal in our exhibition kitchen. Lunch, dinner nightly.

Catering and banquet facilities available at both of our locations.

Pollo Con Formaggi

▼▼▼

Serves 2

2 whole 8 oz chicken breasts,
  boneless, skinless
3 oz sun-dried tomatoes, julienned

1 cup feta cheese, crumbled
4 Tbsp pine nut butter*
  (recipe follows)

Make a cut in each side of chicken breast and fill pockets
with feta cheese and sun-dried tomatoes; reserve some feta and
tomato for a topping.

Grill over mesquite coals, basting chicken lightly with pine
nut butter.

When finished, garnish with feta cheese and strips of sun-
dried tomatoes. Serve with penne (pasta) and grilled summer
squash.

52

Pine Nut Butter

▼▼

Makes approximately 10 servings

1 cup butter
½ cup pine nuts (roasted)
4–6 drops Tabasco
2 Tbsp garlic, pureed

1 Tbsp Worchestershire sauce
1 Tbsp red wine vinegar
2 Tbsp parsley, chopped coarsely

Place roasted pine nuts in a food processor and coarsely grind nuts.

In a mixer combine all ingredients.

The butter is excellent for basting grilled poultry or seafood.

Capellini di Primavera con Verdure

▼▼

Serves 2

14 oz pre-cooked spinach
capellini*
4 cups of mixed vegetables:
   broccoli flowerettes
   chopped red cabbage
   quartered mushrooms
   diced zucchini
   seeded and diced tomatoes

1 tsp garlic, pureed
2 Tbsp olive oil
1 tsp fennel seeds
2 oz white wine
2 Tbsp chilled butter
¼ cup Asiago cheese, shredded
2 sprigs Italian flat parsley

Using a non-stick pan over high heat, heat the olive oil and add all vegetables except tomatoes. Saute for 2 to 3 minutes. Add garlic, wine, fennel and tomatoes to saute pan. Continue to cook until tomatoes are hot.

Heat cooked pasta in hot water, remove, drain thoroughly and add with butter to saute pan.

Toss mixture several times to melt butter. Place in bowls or on large serving platter. Garnish with Italian parsley and Asiago cheese.

* Capellini, very thin pasta, commonly referred to as angel hair, is available at Italian specialty markets and most delis.

Hiram's
At·The·Locks

5300 34th NW
Seattle, Washington 98107
(206) 784-1733

For almost 10 years, Hiram's has given Seattle the kind of casual elegance in dining that makes for a great meal.

Hiram's, named after Hiram Chittenden, designer of the Locks at Shilshole Bay, has a sweeping view of the water that provides quiet entertainment any time of the day.

Hiram's specializes in a variety of fresh seafoods including such favorites as Dungeness Crab Stuffed Prawns, Pesto Salmon and a chef's daily seafood special. Pastas, salads and meats give the menu a balanced approach. A wide selection of Northwest wines is available.

During nice weather, Hiram's large patio overlooking the water is open for lunch, dinner, Sunday brunch or for cocktails and appetizers.

With the relaxed atmosphere inside, the spectacular backdrop of the water, the variety and quality of the menu and the enticement of the patio, Hiram's has established itself as one of Seattle's landmark restaurants.

Mesquite Broiled Salmon with Pesto

▼▼▼

Serves 2

2 8-oz salmon fillets
½ cup olive oil
½ cup salad oil
¼ cup minced garlic

⅓ cup chopped basil
⅓ cup roasted pine nuts
zest of one lemon
salt to taste

In a medium size bowl, add all ingredients together except salmon fillets and pine nuts. Let stand one hour.

Trim salmon fillets to remove any bones or skin which may be present. Chop pine nuts and add to pesto marinade, mix well. Add salmon fillets and let marinate 6 hours under refrigeration, turning salmon fillets over every two hours.

Remove from marinade and grill over mesquite charcoal 3 to 4 minutes on each side. Remove from grill and brush on pesto marinade to taste.

Enjoy!

Select Premium Washington State Wines

North 23501 Highway 101
Hoodsport, Washington 98548
(206) 877-9894

The Hoodsport Winery is a small award-winning winery producing limited bottlings of the finest Washington State wines. You're invited to try our quality Hoodsport wines and Hoodsport Raspberry Wine truffles in our tasting room on beautiful Hood Canal. Open 10:00 – 6:00 daily.

Poached Halibut in Gooseberry Wine

▼▼▼

Serves 2–3

1 cup Hoodsport Gooseberry wine

¼ cup margarine or butter

4-5 Tbsp (Golden Dipt),
    lemon-butter-dill sauce

4 halibut or salmon fillets or
    steaks, or any shell-fish
    combined

Combine first 3 ingredients, simmer about 5 minutes. Add fish and cook until tender or fish begins to flake (about 5 minutes, depending on thickness of fillets or steaks).

This is also excellent using Hoodsport Johannisberg Riesling or Chenin Blanc.

Dosiwallips Scallops

▼▼

Serves 4

1 lb scallops (Bay scallops
  work well)
½ cup Hoodsport Johannisberg
  Riesling
½ cup chicken broth

1-2 Tbsp dijon mustard
¼ cup whipping cream
2 Tbsp butter
2 Tbsp olive oil
½ cup flour

Bring wine and chicken broth to a boil in a saucepan and add mustard. Add whipping cream, bring to boil, then reduce heat and simmer, stirring frequently, about 15 minutes.

In a skillet, heat the butter and oil. Lightly coat scallops with flour, then brown lightly. Pour off the excess oil, add the cream sauce, heat 5 minutes and serve over pasta or rice.

E.B.'s Hood Canal Shrimp

▼▼▼

Serves 4–6

½ cup olive oil

lots of garlic (10 cloves)

3 tsp rock salt

2-3 lbs Hood Canal shrimp or
prawns with shells on

1 lemon

½ cup Hoodsport Gewurztraminer
or Mueller Thurgau

1 bunch fresh parsley

Heat the oil in a large skillet over medium high heat. When the oil is hot add the garlic and cook, stirring, until it begins to look clear in color, around 3 minutes. Add salt and the wine, reduce heat and simmer a couple of minutes to blend flavors.

Add prawns and cook just until prawns are pink, about 5 minutes. Mound shrimp on a large platter and pour the cooking liquid over the shrimp.

Garnish with lemon wedges and fresh parsley.

Horizon's Edge

4530 East Zillah Drive
Zillah, Washingotn 98953
(509) 829-6401

Horizon's Edge Winery is a family-owned winery started in 1985 and located 3 miles east of Zillah, Washington in the famous Yakima Valley. The 16-acre vineyard was planted in 1985, and produced its first crop of Chardonnay, Pinot Noir and Muscat Canelli in 1988.

Tom Campbell is the proprietor and man behind the winemaking. Trained at the University of California at Davis in enology and viti-culture, he has worked at several different wineries, including Jekel, Shiloh, and Ste. Michelle Winery, learning all he could about winemaking. Following his work at these wineries, he became winemaker for several Washington state wineries including Covey Run, Stewart and Tucker Cellars. In 1984 he and his parents started the Mission Mountain Winery, Montana's first bonded winery.

The Winery currently produces approximately 2000 cases of wine a year. The wines produced include: Barrel Fermented Char-donnay, Pinot Noir, Cabernet Sauvignon, Muscat Canelli and Champagne.

The Vineyard is managed by Pat Smith (also our tasting room guru). Pat is a member of the first graduating class of the Yakima Valley Community College's viticulture program. He is responsible for the personal manicuring and training of our 20-acre estate vine-yard, consisting of Chardonnay, Pinot Noir, Cabernet Sauvignon and Muscat Canelli.

You are welcome to use our picnic facilities.

Ginger Snapper with Saffron Rice

▼▼

Serves 6–8

4 lbs fresh red snapper

Marinade:

2 oz fresh ginger

1 clove fresh garlic

2 oz light soy sauce

4 oz Horizon's Edge Chardonnay*
or white table wine

Saffron rice:

1½ cups rice, long grain

¼ tsp saffron

½ tsp salt

2 cups water

Combine fresh chopped or grated ginger, light soy, wine and crushed garlic in bowl. Put fish in the marinade for 2 to 4 hours.

Prepare rice about 20-30 minutes before you are ready to grill the fish. Bring water to a boil in a medium saucepan. Add rice, saffron, and salt. Reduce heat to low, stir rice once, cover and cook 20-30 minutes.

Grill marinated snapper on gas or charcoal grill until it flakes and fish is opaque. Brush fish with marinade occasionally. Serve with Horizon's Edge Muscat Canelli and saffron rice.

*Horizon's Edge wines are available at Olsen's stores.

Rainier Cherry Sauce

▼▼

Makes 1 quart

1 lb Rainier cherries*

1 oz white wine vinegar

1 oz cane sugar

¼ tsp ascorbic acid

Split and pit cherries and place in blender. Add vinegar, sugar and ascorbic acid. Puree until smooth.

Use as a condiment for oriental meat dishes, barbequed pork, beef satay, chicken wings, etc.

*Rainier cherries are available at Pike Place Market.

HUNAN HARBOR

2040 Westlake Avenue
Seattle, Washington 98109
(206) 286-1688

First there was the Hunan Restaurant in Portland. Then Hunan Gardens in Bellevue. Now the Hunan tradition has arrived in Seattle! Located on the western shore of glistening Lake Union, Hunan Harbor offers Seattleites a unique and exotic dining experience featuring authentic Chinese cuisine from the central provinces of Mainland China.

The cuisine of Hunan celebrates the red pepper indigenous to China's inland regions. This pepper stimulates the palate, allowing it to accommodate and enjoy a greater number of flavors at one time. Once the "hot" taste has passed, the diner experiences a certain mellowness followed by the many flavor characteristics of Hunan cuisine.

We have deliberately chosen some of the most delectable and authentic specialties of Hunan Province for your dining pleasure.

You will enjoy the cuisine of Hunan, an experience in a rare and classic culture – a stimulation of the mind and palate.

Located in the newly remodeled China House Trade Center, Hunan Harbor offers sweeping views of Seattle's busiest waterway, a full-service cocktail lounge, a complete giftshop and art gallery.

65

Moo Shu Pork

▼▼▼

Serves 4

8 oz pork, shredded
3 Tbsp oil
½ head cabbage, shredded
2 Tbsp soy sauce
4 oz shredded bamboo shoots
½ tsp salt

2 oz tree mushrooms*
¼ tsp white pepper
3 eggs, beaten
⅛ tsp monosodium glutimate
10 2" pieces green onion
3 Tbsp Hoisin Sauce
flour tortillas

Heat the wok or fry pan, put in 1 Tbsp of oil, stir fry the eggs, remove from pan and set aside.

Add 2 Tbsp of oil to pan and put the pork in, stir fry for 2 minutes. Add and stir fry remaining ingredients for another 7 minutes, add eggs. Wrap filling in soft flour tortillas or fill pocket bread.

* Tree mushrooms: small, dried, charred-looking fungus about 1" long and irregularly shaped. Expands to 5 or 6 times its original size, becomes brown and gelatinous. Available at Asian markets or Uwajimaya.

401 NE Northlake Way
(on Lake Union)
Seattle, Washington 98105
(206) 632-0767

Ivar's Salmon House is a familiar landmark on the northeast shore of Lake Union. This beautiful cedar replica of a Pacific Northwest Indian longhouse offers generous views of passing boats and fabulous Seattle skyline view to the south. The Salmon House is famous for its succulent Alder Smoked Salmon, barbecued over a fragrant, open-pit alder fire, but they also serve a wide range of other delicious entrees including Alder Smoked Black Cod, Prawns, Prime Rib, and Barbecued Chicken. The outdoor Seafood Bar provides take-out service or casual lakeside dining, and the Sunday Buffet Brunch offers plenty of traditional breakfast fare, along with a variety of alder smoked seafood.

Winner of the 1986 and 1987 Business Executive Dining Award as one of the 100 top restaurants in the country for favorable business entertaining, the Salmon House is also a member of the Seattle Historical Society and home to one of the city's finest Northwest Indian photo and artifact collections.

Alder Smoked Salmon

▼▼▼

Serves 2

1 lb (2 8-oz servings) salmon filet, boned, with skin left on

Marinade:

2 Tbsp cottonseed oil

¼ tsp black pepper

1 small garlic clove, pureed

⅛ tsp salt

1 Tbsp lemon juice

Lemon Butter:

1 Tbsp lemon juice

1 tsp finely grated lemon peel

⅛ tsp white pepper

½ cup butter or margarine

Combine marinade ingredients. Place salmon in bowl with marinade. Cover container with plastic wrap and marinate in refrigerator at least 8 hours.

Build fire in barbeque pit using alderwood. When wood is burning without flames, place salmon on rack, skin side up. Broil the salmon 4" to 6" from the heat source for 5 to 7 minutes. Turn over, skin side down, basting salmon with lemon butter. Continue cooking about 7 to 10 minutes or until done.

Serve with Ivar's tartar sauce.

Note: The recipes for Ivar's have been adapted from the large, open, alderwood pit at the Salmon House to fit your small hibachi or backyard grill. We suggest you line your grill with foil, then with charcoal. You can buy alderwood chips and that's our top choice, but hickory chips will do, too. Soak the wood in water for an hour so the chips smoke, not burn. When your coals are hot, place wood chips on top for a smoky flavor.

THE KALEENKA
A RUSSIAN RESTAURANT

1933 1st Avenue
Seattle, Washington 98101
(206) 728-1278

It's a long way from the Ukraine in the Soviet Union to the Pike Place market in Seattle, but that's how far Lydia Venichenko-Barrett has come to prepare her genuine Russian food for the people of Seattle.

For the past twelve years The Kaleenka has served strictly Russian food at its finest, dishes originating from the Ukraine to Siberia. Venichenko-Barrett, born and raised in the Ukraine, is the owner of the only place in Seattle you can find a real Russian dish and a quick lesson in Soviet culture.

Lunch and dinner menus include such delicacies as Beef Stroganoff, cabbage rolls and many varieties of Ragu. All dinners are served with borshch or a tossed salad and a choice of brown rice, roasted buckwheat or Russian pan fried potatoes.

The Kaleenka serves a delicious variety of desserts and espresso drinks. There is also an interesting selection of imported beers and wines from Yugoslavia, Poland, Hungary, Norway and Denmark.

The combination of the ethnic decor, the savory, authentic food and the staff, who all speak Russian, makes for a wonderful Russian evening right here in Seattle.

Piroshky

▼▼

Dough:
1½ pkgs dry yeast
¼ cup warm water
2 Tbsp sugar
1 tsp salt
1½ cups milk
1 egg
¼ cup oil or butter
4-5 cups flour

Filling:
1 med onion, chopped
2 lbs ground round beef
1 clove garlic, minced
salt
pepper

A pirozhok is singular for piroshky. Both words derive from the Russian word *pin*, which means feast. Piroshky are a miniature feast.

Dissolve yeast in water. Let stand 10 minutes.

In large bowl combine flour, sugar and salt. Make a well in flour and add milk, egg, oil and yeast. Combine to make a soft dough. Knead about 10 minutes. Let rise one half hour to one hour.

Brown chopped onion and garlic. In separate pan, brown ground beef. Season with salt, pepper, garlic and onion. Cool meat mixture and remove solidified fat.

Pinch a golf-ball sized piece of dough, flatten with fingers or roll out to ⅛" thickness. Place 2 Tbsp filling in center and bring opposite edges of circle together and pinch securely. (The traditional shape is a plump center with tapering edges.)

Let piroshky rise seam side down, 30 minutes.

Heat oven to 350°. Brush piroshky with egg yolk and bake till golden brown. They may also be deep fried.

Borshch

Serves 4-6

1 med onion, chopped
1 to 3 carrots, grated
1 to 2 beets, grated
1 potato, cubed
2 cups coarsely cut cabbage
½ green pepper, chopped
½ stalk celery, chopped
1 clove garlic

1 cup tomato juice
3 Tbsp oil
3 to 4 cups water
salt
pepper
fresh or dried dill (garnish)
sour cream (garnish)

This is a traditional Ukranian soup, served at Lent without meat.

Brown onion, carrots, and beets separately in 1 Tbsp of oil each. Set aside.

In saucepan bring 3 to 4 cups water to boiling and add remaining vegetables. Bring back to boiling and add onions, carrots and beets. Cook till vegetables are tender.

Add salt and pepper to taste, and tomato juice.

Serve piping hot with 1 tsp chopped fresh dill and a dollop of sour cream in each bowl. Accompany soup with a good rye bread.

Karam's

340 15th Avenue East
Seattle, Washington 98112
(206) 324-2370

Lebanese hospitality is quite demonstrative, and we offer our guests the best food in a comfortable atmosphere. This custom is easily understood by everyone who dines at Karam's.

There is a proverb to the effect that the measure of a guest's regard for his host is the amount of food which he eats – "al akl'ala kadd el mahabeh" – "the food equals the affection."

Karam's professes this concept with original recipes prepared in our kitchen with love, quality and freshness. We serve tender, juicy marinated char-broiled chicken, lamb shish-kebob covered with garlic sauce, fish or spicy falafil, crispy on the outside, chewy inside, drizzled with garlicky tahini sauce. We also serve baba ghannouj, hummus, tabbouleh and, on occasion, our special lebaneh or the ever-popular favorite, stuffed char-broiled kebbeh, Thursday through Saturday. We also have imported beers and wines from Lebanon, Morocco and Algeria. Drop by for an experience you and your taste buds will long remember.

Booza Bi Ma'es Zahr
Orange Blossom Ice Cream

▼▼▼

Serves 8–10

3¾ cups milk
1¼ cups cream
1¼ cups sugar (or less)
1 tsp sahlab*

¼ tsp mustikah*
1 Tbsp orange blossom water*
chopped pistachios

Dissolve sahlab in a small portion of the milk. Pour remaining milk in saucepan with cream and sugar. Bring to a boil. Add milk and sahlab mixture to boiled milk, stirring occasionally.

Pulverize mustikah with one Tbsp sugar, using a mortar and pestle, to a fine powder. Stir into boiled milk.

Simmer over low heat for fifteen minutes, stirring occasionally. Add orange blossom water. Remove from heat. Beat well with spoon.

Pour into ice tray and cover with foil. Freeze. Beat 3 to 4 times by hand during freezing to break up ice crystals.

Transfer ice cream to refrigerator 20 minutes before serving.

Sprinkle with pistachios. Serve with Turkish coffee. Enjoy!

*Sahlab: similar to corn starch. *Mustikah: resin from a pine tree. Sahlab, mustikah, Turkish coffee and orange blossom water may be purchased at Pacific Food Importers.

Farareej Mashwieh Bi Toum
Charbroiled Chicken with Garlic Sauce

Serves 2

1 whole chicken or 2 halves
12 cloves garlic
4 tsp salt
½ tsp pepper

½ cup wine vinegar
½ cup pure extra virgin olive oil
1 lemon
sumac for garnish*

Clean split chicken thoroughly. Wipe dry.

Crush four cloves garlic, using a mortar and pestle, with two tsp salt until a paste is formed. Add wine vinegar, ¼ cup olive oil and ¼ tsp pepper.

Marinate chicken in garlic mixture overnight.

Broil chicken over charcoal or gas.

Drizzle with garlic sauce (recipe follows). Sprinkle with sumac, and serve over rice. Enjoy!

Garlic Sauce: Pulverize 8 cloves garlic with two tsp salt to a paste. Add gradually ¼ cup olive oil and ¼ tsp pepper. Squeeze juice from one lemon. Add to mixture. This sauce should be velvety smooth.

---

*Sumac: dried, crushed red berries of a species of sumac tree. Sour lemony in flavor. Available at Pacific Food Importers.

Adas Bi Haamud
Lentils with Swiss Chard, Lemon and Garlic

▼▼▼

Serves 6

1½ cups lentils

1 bunch Swiss chard (red or white), with stems

1 large onion

½ cup pure extra virgin olive oil

1 stalk celery

5 cloves garlic

2 tsp salt

¼ tsp pepper

½ cup lemon juice (2 to 3 lemons)

sumac*

Wash lentils well. Drain overnight.

Wash and remove any small stones in morning. Boil lentils in 3 quarts water until tender. Add more water if necessary. Wash and chop Swiss chard leaves, stems and celery. Add to lentils.

Fry chopped onion in olive oil until yellow. Crush garlic with salt using mortar and pestle. Add fried onions, crushed garlic and lemon juice to lentils. Simmer to a thick rich soup.

Sprinkle with sumac. Serve with pita bread. Enjoy!

* Sumac: dried, crushed red berries of a species of sumac tree. Sour lemony in flavor. Available at Pacific Food Importers.

Kaspar's
by the Bay

2701 First Avenue
Seattle, Washington 98121
(206) 441-4805

A newcomer to the Seattle restaurant scene, Kaspar's by the Bay brings an exciting fresh influence to Pacific Northwest Cuisine. Formerly presiding as Executive Chef over La Reserve, the Houston Four Seasons Inn on the Park Hotel's showcase restaurant is chef/owner Kaspar Donier. Kaspar combines the Northwest style with classic French, Oriental and Southwestern regional techniques... resulting in unique and adventurous fare at Kaspar's by the Bay.

Overlooking the expanse of Elliott Bay, diners are treated to the ever-changing scene of harbor activity, and on a clear day, can enjoy a breathtaking vista of Mt. Rainier, as well as the rugged Olympic Range. The view from Kaspar's by the Bay is indeed unparalleled in Seattle.

Open Monday through Friday for lunch and dinner, Saturday dinner and Sunday brunch, Kaspar's by the Bay is the perfect choice for all occasions, including the special event which requires private dining accommodations. Kaspar's has three private banquet rooms, which will comfortably serve 120 sit-down dinner guests or 175 reception guests.

Zucchini Bisque with Crabmeat

Serves 4–6

1 med onion, diced
2 Tbsp butter
3 med zucchini, diced
1 potato, diced
5 cups chicken stock

1 sprig fresh thyme
pinch each of salt and pepper
2 cups heavy (whipping) cream
½ cup lump crabmeat
chives

Fry onion in butter until transparent. Add zucchini and potatoes; fry a few minutes.

Add stock, thyme and seasonings. Season 30 minutes. Transfer to blender container and blend until smooth. Return to pot.

Add cream and crabmeat. Bring to a boil. Serve. Garnish with cut chives.

Chicken with Green Asparagus Coulis

Serves 4

4 6-oz chicken breast halves
dash of seasoning mix (salt,
    pepper, paprika and nutmeg)
¼ cup olive oil
1 lb fresh green asparagus

1 garlic clove, chopped
1 shallot, chopped
1 oz (2 Tbsp) butter
1 cup chicken stock

Season chicken breasts with seasoning mix. Pan-fry the breasts in olive oil until golden brown.

Cut 2 inches off top and 1 inch off bottom of the asparagus. Discard the bottom part. Cook the asparagus tips in a small amount of salted water about 4 minutes, then immediately plunge into cold water to stop cooking and preserve color. The tips will be used as garnish on the plate.

Saute the garlic and shallot in butter and add the middle part of the asparagus. Add chicken stock and simmer, covered, about 5 minutes. Process well in blender. Season to taste.

Pour the asparagus puree on bottom of plate and place chicken breast on top. Garnish with the warm asparagus tips and chopped fresh dill.

Wild Mushroom Raviolis with Chive Sauce

▼▼▼

Serves 4 as an appetizer

12 wonton wrappers (rounds, 3"
in diameter)

2 oz shitake mushrooms, finely
sliced

3 oz enokie mushrooms, finely
sliced

2 oz oyster mushrooms, finely
sliced

2 Tbsp butter, melted

pinch each of salt, tarragon and
rosemary

1 shallot

⅓ cup white wine such as Riesling

¾ cup heavy (whipping) cream

1 bunch fresh chives

Wonton wrappers are a handy and clever substitute for pasta.
Boil wonton wrappers, 6 at a time, like pasta in large pot of
boiling water; 2 or 3 minutes. Drain and cool.

Saute mushrooms in frying pan with butter and season with
herbs. Simmer about 5 minutes until all mushroom liquid is
evaporated. Remove mushrooms from pan and let cool.

Place a Tbsp of mushroom mixture in the middle of each won
ton and fold all sides of the wrapper up to the middle, pinch to
seal.

Steam on a rack over a little simmering water in a covered
pan or wok 3 minutes.

Place shallot and white wine in a saucepan. Let cook down
until reduced by half. Add chicken stock and cream.

Let mixture reduce again by half or until desired consistency
is achieved. Add chives at the last minute.

Arrange 3 raviolis on a plate and cover with sauce.

15740 Redmond Way
Redmond, Washington 98052
(206) 883-HULA

Lahaina Louies opened its doors on New Year's Eve, 1987. Founded by Doug Morrison, the concept of a Hawaiian restaurant has proven to be very successful on the Eastside. With tropical decor and the spirit of aloha abounding, Lahaina Louies serves excellent food for lunch, dinner and Sunday brunch.

The menu is extensive and includes entrees such as prime rib, steaks, the famous azekka ribs, pasta and wok dishes, salads and the popular choices of fish flown in from Hawaii. The lunch menu offers selections of sandwiches, burgers, Polynesian entrees and salads. Aloha Sunday brunch buffet and menu is offered weekly. A children's menu is available.

Shrimp Tahitian

▼▼

Serves 4

8 oz margarine
36 prawns (21/25 count per lb)
2 oz cubed white onion
8 oz sherry
2 tsp garlic powder
1 tsp salt

1 tsp pepper
1 cup diced tomatoes
2 tsp chopped parsley
2 cups Parmesan cheese
8 oz mushrooms

Saute prawns and white onions over medium heat in butter till half done. Add sherry, garlic, salt and pepper. Cook till almost done.

Add mushrooms, tomatoes and 1 cup of Parmesan cheese. Stir till cheese melts. Sprinkle remaining cheese on top of mixture and place in oven to brown.

Serve in shallow casserole dish, topped with chopped parsley.

Chicken Oriental

▼▼

Serves 4

6 oz sesame oil

24 oz ¼" cut chicken strips

8 oz broccoli

6 oz white onions

4 oz green pepper strips

4 oz red pepper strips

6 oz pea pods

8 oz mushrooms

6 oz carrots

6 oz celery

12 pcs baby corn

4 oz water chestnuts

4 oz sherry

4 oz oyster sauce

8 oz blackbean sauce

1 cup bean sprouts

Heat sesame oil in wok till hot. Add chicken and stir until three-quarters done.

Add mushrooms, carrots, celery, baby corn, water chestnuts, and stir till vegetables are barely cooked. Add sherry, oyster sauce and black bean sauce. Cook till chicken is done and veggies are *al dente*.

Stir in bean sprouts and serve in a bed of rice. Sprinkle sesame seeds over top of dish.

Le Monde

1809 Queen Anne Avenue North
Seattle, Washington 98109
(206) 286-1010

Le Monde offers an alternative home delivery service to couples and families who are interested in a choice other than Pizza or Chinese deliveries.

Le Monde was established by Dirk E. Fisher and Maria Ghaly in early 1988. Both are trained in their craft in international settings. Their menu offers seven choices of cuisine from around the world (hence the name): Spanish, Italian, French, Greek, Indian, Oriental and Tex-Mex. These are complete dinners that include appetizers, salads and main course. They arrive at your door in 30–45 minutes ready to eat in a special container.

The service initially covered the Queen Anne/Magnolia area is now expanded to Capitol Hill, Fremont and Wallingford.

House Chutney

▼▼▼

Makes approximately 2 quarts

1 lb *white raisins*

1 lb *Turkish apricots, coarsely chopped*

4 sm *oranges, coarsely chopped*

4 *lemons, coarsely chopped*

4 *limes, coarsely chopped*

3 med *onions, chopped more finely than citrus*

1 *red pepper, chopped medium fine*

1 *green pepper, chopped medium fine*

2 lg *tomatoes, chopped*

2 *carrots, grated*

2 3" *cinnamon sticks*

2 Tbsp *salt*

3 cups *malt vinegar*

2 lbs *brown sugar*

2 Tbsp *molasses (a good substitute for Indian jaggary)*

6 Tbsp *fresh ginger, finely grated*

3 Tbsp *crushed garlic*

1 tsp *ground clove*

½ cup *fresh cilantro (chop leaves and tender stems only)*

1 cup *vegetable oil*

4 tsp *dry mustard*

Chop all fruits and vegetables. Combine in heavy pan, or wok, all fruit, onions, pepper, vegetables, vinegar, salt, and cinnamon. Bring to a boil over medium heat, stirring very frequently.

When mixture boils add brown sugar and molasses and continue to cook for five minutes. Lower heat to medium and add ginger, garlic and cloves. Cook for five more minutes, adding cilantro, then remove from heat.

In a small cast iron skillet heat oil until it begins to smoke. Remove from heat and add dry mustard. Add oil/mustard mixture to fruit/vegetable mixture (caution, oil will sputter when it contacts fruit mixture). Stir and cool to room temperature.

Chutney will keep up to three months under refrigeration.

Basmati Rice

▼▼

Serves 6

2 cups Basmati rice*	¼ cup golden raisins
3 Tbsp oil	3 cups water
1 lg onion, chopped	salt
½ tsp tumeric	½ tsp masala*

Wash rice thoroughly in 3 changes of water, then soak for 5 minutes and let drain and dry for 5 minutes.

Heat oil in skillet, add onion and masala and fry until the onion is golden. Add rice and fry for 10 minutes until it turns translucent.

Pour in 3 cups boiling water, add tsp salt, turmeric and simmer over low heat for 10 minutes. Turn off heat and let stand, covered, for 5 minutes until all moisture has been absorbed and the grains of rice are separate and tender. Add raisins.

* Basmati rice is a long grain white rice of very high quality, grown in India and Pakistan, that is distinguished by its nutty flavor and aroma. Available at Pike Place Market and Larry's Market. Masala: spices and other seasonings slow roasted, then ground together to provide the base for an Indian sauce. Available at MarketSpice, The Souk or Le Monde.

Tandoori Chicken

Serves 4

8 whole chicken legs, skinned
3 Tbsp lemon juice
salt
1 lemon, sliced
1 sm onion, thinly sliced
1 cup plain yogurt
Tandoori seasoning paste:
1 tsp ground coriander
1 Tbsp onion powder

1 Tbsp ground ginger
1 Tbsp garlic powder
2 Tbsp paprika
½ tsp ground cumin
1 tsp masala*
1 Tbsp ground cardamom
½ tsp red chili pepper
1 tsp tumeric

For Tandoori seasoning paste: mix all dry ingredients listed under seasoning paste with enough water and about 2 Tbsp salad oil to make a thick paste.

To prepare chicken: make half inch slashes in the skinned whole chicken legs with a very sharp knife. Rub in lemon juice and sprinkle with salt. Mix 2 Tbsp water with yogurt and spoon over the legs. Brush on the seasoning paste, making sure to coat both sides well. Cover and refrigerate in the marinade overnight. Reserve remaining Tandoori sauce.

Brush on remaining paste just before baking or barbequeing. Cook legs on an oven rack across a roasting pan in a 425° oven about 45 minutes till juices run clear; or BBQ on outdoor grill for 30 minutes over medium hot coals and keep turning and basting with any remaining paste.

Garnish with lemon and onion slices.

* Masala: spices and other seasonings slow roasted, then ground together to provide the base for an Indian sauce. Available at MarketSpice, The Souk or Le Monde.

MARKET CAFE

THE WESTIN HOTEL
Seattle

The Westin Hotel
1900 Fifth Avenue
Seattle, Washington 98101

A market-style dining room patterned after Seattle's historic Pike Place Market, offers daily seafood specials, fresh produce, fifty varieties of domestic and imported beer and a special children's menu.

Market Cafe Pacific Seafood Operetta

▼▼

Serves 4–6

¼ cup vegetable oil
½ cup finely chopped onions
1 garlic clove, crushed
⅔ cup diced green pepper
1¼ cup diced celery
4 tomatoes, peeled and seeded
½ tsp salt, pepper

2 Dungeness crabs (total weight about 2¼ lbs)
¾ lb clams or scallops
2¼ lb mussels
1 Tbsp chopped parsley
2 cups St Michael chablis

Heat the oil in a pan and lightly fry the onions and garlic. Add the green peppers and celery and simmer for 5–6 minutes. Add the tomatoes, and season to taste. Add only the cracked claws and the body meat from the crabs. Add the clams (in shell), scrub the mussels under running water, debeard and add to the pan. Sprinkle with parsley, and pour on the wine.

Cook over low heat, on the stove or in the oven, for about 15 minutes. Discard any clams or mussels that have not opened, and serve.

Yakima Valley Pear Tart with Almond Cream

Serves 6

Pastry:
2 cups all purpose flour
1 cup granulated sugar
pinch of salt
⅔ cup unsalted butter, cut into
   small pieces
1 egg
Almond Cream:

¾ cup unsalted butter, softened
1½ cups powdered almonds
2 eggs
1 Tbsp rum
Assembly:
4 pears (about 1½ lb) cooked
   in syrup
apricot jelly

Prepare the pastry. Place flour, sugar, and salt in a food processor. Add pieces of butter and process until blended, about 15 seconds. Add egg and process until pastry masses into a ball, about 30 seconds. Turn out onto a floured work surface and form into a neat round. Wrap in plastic and refrigerate at least one hour.

Prepare the almond cream. Using an electric mixer, blend together softened butter and powdered almonds in a bowl. One at a time, add eggs; add rum; mix well, cover and refrigerate.

Assemble the tart. Preheat the oven to 400 degrees. Roll out the pastry and line a 11 to 12 inch removable bottom tart pan. Chill for 30 minutes before filling. Cut cooked pears lengthwise into quarters, removing the cores and seeds. Smooth the almond cream over bottom of the tart shell. Arrange quartered pears on the top in a star pattern.

Bake for 30 minutes. Unmold the tart when cool. Glaze the top with melted apricot jelly if desired.

Rib Steak Ten Plus Ten
with Walla Walla Sweet Onions

▼▼▼

Serves 4

2 lbs boneless rib steaks

6 Tbsp butter in all

2 med Walla Walla sweet onions, minced

⅓ cup red wine vinegar

½ cup light, dry red wine

½ tsp peppercorns, slightly crushed

several sprigs fresh thyme

1 rounded tsp tomato paste

coarse salt

1-2 Tbsp peanut oil

2 Tbsp mixed, chopped chervil, parsley, tarragon

Melt 3 Tbsp of the butter in a heavy 1-quart saucepan. Add onions, and cook them for 5 minutes over a low heat, stirring frequently. The onions should be soft but not browned. Add vinegar to the onions, and cook them over high heat until all the liquid has evaporated. Quickly add the wine, pepper, thyme, tomato paste, and a good pinch of coarse salt. Simmer the sauce gently over low heat for 20 minutes. Remove the sprigs of thyme if fresh was used, and, stirring briskly, incorporate 2 Tbsp of butter, a little at a time. Taste for seasoning.

Sprinkle the steaks lightly with salt and pepper. Melt 1 Tbsp of butter with as much oil as needed to coat a heavy frying pan. When the butter sizzles, and the oil begins to smoke, add the meat and cook it quickly for 10 seconds on each side.

Spoon the hot onion sauce over the meat, and sprinkle it with the chopped fresh herbs.

Metropolitan Grill

820 2nd Avenue
Seattle, Washington 98104
(206) 624-3287

Located in the heart of Seattle's downtown financial and business center, "The Met" (as it has affectionately come to be known) is very simply the best steak house in town.

Nobody better than Seattle Times restaurant critic John Hinterberger could describe the experience. "A downtown business person's restaurant for lunch which becomes a steak house for dinner – arguably the best in town."

The Metropolitan Grill features dry-cured and 28-day aging of its meat. The beef is carefully broiled over the "iron wood of the world," imported Mexican mesquite charcoal, to further enhance its flavor. The sight of a fabulous Porterhouse, Delmonico or Chateaubriand for two, never was more appealing or flavorful. And there's always Fresh King Salmon, Veal Parmigiana, or extra thick Veal Chops to tempt your taste buds.

While beef is the mainstay of the Met, the lunch menu features the freshest pastas, salads, fish and homemade soups. The dinner menu is enhanced by a fresh sheet featuring the latest catch of Northwest seafood.

The 1987 award by Northwest Gourmet Magazine as the best business lunch, only adds to what Seattleites already know – the Metropolitan Grill is the best in town.

Tenderloin Steak Sandwich

▼▼▼

Serves 5

1 lb beef tenderloin medallions
5 kaiser dollar-sized buns
1 oz steak seasoning
5 Tbsp grade AA butter

1 tsp fresh minced garlic
½ tsp chopped parsley
½ minced green onion
½ tsp granulated onion

Soften butter. Add minced garlic, parsley, green onion and granulated onion to butter and blend thoroughly. Butter kaiser dollar buns. Season tenderloin medallions, to taste. Mesquite broil 1 to 2 minutes per side (preferred rare to medium rare).

Serve hot on Kaiser buns.

"Where fresh seafood
comes ashore."®

10426 NE Northup Way
Kirkland, Washington 98033
(206) 827-2722

Newport Bay Restaurant is located between Kirkland and
Bellevue. Newport Bay specializes in the daily preparation of fresh
seafood. Our daily menu features fresh salmon, ling cod, sole,
Pacific snapper and mahi-mahi. Chef Les Martin also writes a daily
fresh and special sheet which highlights the availability of the fresh
catch-of-the-day.

Open daily for lunch and dinner, Newport Bay offers a wide
variety of menu items including salads, pasta dishes, chicken and
beef dinners, sandwiches and gourmet hamburgers. A children's
menu is also available. Every Sunday Newport Bay offers its
signature Sunday brunch.

Shrimp Curry Salad

▼▼

Serves 6

1 lb fresh bay shrimp	½ banana, sliced	Garnish:
½ cup diced celery	3 Tbsp honey	1 orange wheel
¼ cup diced onion	zest of 1 orange	1 parsley sprig
1 cup mayonnaise	1 oz orange juice	½ oz green onions
¼ cup pineapple	1 Tbsp curry powder	1 green leaf
¼ cup raisins	1 Tbsp fresh butter	3 oz salad mix
1 mango, cleaned & diced		6 oz curry salad mix
		1 sm cold salad plate

On low heat in a sauce pan, add the butter and the curry powder, just until the butter is hot (this will bring out the flavor in the curry). Set aside and allow to cool.

Take the mango, peel it and remove the seed. Mince the onion and the celery. Set aside. Fresh pineapple is preferred, but canned chopped pineapple can be used. The orange needs to be zested and juiced, and the banana is to be sliced.

Rinse the shrimp under cold water. Combine all ingredients, and mix thoroughly. Allow to set for one hour for flavors to blend.

Line green leaf on salad plate, add green salad mix, then shrimp salad, garnish with orange twist, parsley sprig, and green onions.

The Other Place

96 Union
Seattle, Washington 98101
(206) 623-7340

The Other Place was our first restaurant to champion the possibilities of Northwest products, and developed the basis for Northwest cuisine. The quality of the base products became a signature and principle behind the restaurant, resulting in the formation of a game farm, fish company, vegetable farms, and a veal farm, thus introducing an entirely new understanding of quality.

The Other Place produces a menu which is a moving image of the Northwest, changing seasonally. Seafood has long been a focus of attention at this restaurant, yet our real specialty has been flavor, presented with clarity and regularity. We welcome everyone to enjoy The Other Place.

Italian Sausage

▼▼

Serves 13

fresh pork shoulder, boneless
1.5 oz salt
½ oz ground black pepper
¾ oz whole fennel seed
2 tsp paprika

1 Tbsp red chili flakes
1 Tbsp minced garlic
½ oz fresh basil, minced
1 cup shaved ice
approx. 6' of 31/35 mm hog casings*

Cut the pork into 1" cubes. Mix all seasonings into the meat. Disperse evenly and thoroughly. Cover and place under refrigeration.

Set up meat grinder using the large hole disc.

Rinse the casings thoroughly under running tap water. Hold the casings "water balloon style" under the faucet and rinse interior of the casing thoroughly also. Let sit in shallow bowl with water.

Grind seasoned pork twice and again return to refrigerator.

Set up meat grinder with the sausage making attachment. Slide casing onto end and push the full length on until you've reached the other end of the casing and tie a double knot.

Distribute the crushed ice evenly throughout the sausage mixture. The ice will serve as a lubricant of sorts and help to keep the meat from sticking in the grinder as you are filling the casings.

Next, fill the feed tray on the meat grinder and begin filling the casing. Hold the casing onto the fill spout with one hand and use the other hand to feed the meat mixture into the grinder. As the casing begins to fill you can control the tightness of the sausage by how fast you allow it to slide from the fill spout. Use your thumb and forefinger to control that and to feel

98

whether the sausage casing is being filled too tightly or too loosely. After all the meat has been filled into a casing, twist or tie the sausages into desired lengths.

Store under refrigeration overnight. Freeze any part of the sausages you do not use within 3 days. Before cooking, prick with a fork a couple times to prevent the sausages rupturing when cooking. Use any method to cook.

* Hog casings are available from Lennon Packing Co.

Spicy Tomato Sauce

▼▼

Serves 13

2 large onions

2 red bell peppers

2 green bell peppers

1 head of garlic

2 32-oz cans peeled, seeded and
  diced tomatoes in juice

1 6-oz can tomato paste

4 cups red wine

¼ cup lemon juice

1 Tbsp sugar

¼ cup thyme

½ cup oregano

¼ cup basil

salt, black pepper and red chili
  flakes to taste

Coarsely chop onions, peppers and garlic.

Saute onions and peppers until translucent and add garlic. Add tomato paste and deglaze with red wine. Reduce. Add tomatoes and cook over low heat for 2–3 hours.

Add sugar, lemon and seasonings. Puree in a food mill or food processor. Return to heat and serve ladled over Italian Sausage.

Central Office Building
15 Oregon Avenue, Suite 106
Tacoma, Washington 98409

Each year at the Bite of Seattle as well as at our franchise locations throughout the United States, Picolo's prepares and serves thousands of gourmet espresso beverages. One of our most popular drinks is our Mocha Plus. It contains the rich, chocolate taste of our award-winning caffe mocha beverage plus a hint of one of our popular gourmet fruit and nut flavorings. Your choice – hot or iced!

Picolo's Mocha Plus, Iced or Hot

▼▼▼

Serves 1

espresso
2 oz Hershey's dark chocolate
   syrup
crushed ice

1 oz Picolo's fruit or nut flavoring
cold milk
whipped cream
grated chocolate

For iced mocha: prepare one or more shots of espresso using fresh Picolo's Premium Blend espresso beans. It is very important that you use only the freshest beans and that they are ground properly. Refrigerate until the espresso is ice cold.

Pour 2 ounces of Hershey's dark chocolate syrup into a tall glass. Fill glass with crushed ice. Pour in one or two shots of iced espresso, depending on your taste. Add one ounce of your favorite Picolo's fruit or nut flavoring. Hazelnut, Almond (Orgeat), Mint, Vanilla, and Raspberry are the most requested. Fill glass with cold milk and mix thoroughly.

For hot mocha: Prepare one or two shots of espresso as above, using only fresh Picolo's Premium Blend espresso beans.

Pour 1 ounce of Hershey's dark chocolate syrup and one ounce of your favorite Picolo's gourmet fruit or nut flavoring into an 8-10 oz coffee mug. Add one or two shots of freshly prepared espresso, to taste. Steam fresh cold milk until hot and pour into mug. Mix thoroughly. Top with fresh whipped cream and grated chocolate.

PRESTON

WINE CELLARS

502 E Vineyard Drive
Pasco, Washington 99301
(509) 545-1990

Preston Wine Cellars, located in the fertile irrigated farmlands of Washington State's Columbia Basin, is one of the Pacific Northwest's most promising wine growing endeavors. Eastern Washington, climatically similar to Northern Europe, is fast gaining recognition as a major production area for wine grapes of exceptional varietal character and balance. Bill and Joann Preston were among the pioneer families who early on recognized the potential of this unexploited area. In 1972 the first vineyard of 50 acres was planted and was increased by 131 acres in 1979.

In the spring of 1976 ground was broken for the winery building and the first crush got underway in late September of that same year. By the fall of 1977 Preston's dream was completed by adding a tasting bar, retail sales room and gift shop. The elevated tasting-room, nestled in the estate vineyards, is uniquely decorated in cedar with a handcrafted bar and personalized furniture created by Brent Preston. Visitors may sip four wines of the 14 award-winning wines on the tasting bar daily, either inside or outside on the over-hanging deck, while enjoying a panoramic view of the vineyards and surrounding countryside.

You may wish to go on a self-guided tour by meandering through hallways containing awards from present and past years and viewing rooms which overlook rows of stainless steel tanks, French oak cooperage, and the mechanized bottling line.

The Prestons and staff cordially invite you to visit the winery year around. We are open daily from 10:00 am, to 5:30 pm, except major holidays. We are located 5 miles north of Pasco on Highway 395. Watch for our sign on the east side of the highway.

103

Stuffed Wine Mushrooms

▼▼

Serves 2

12 medium sized mushrooms
½ cup onions, diced
4 Tbsp butter
½ cup celery, diced

1 tsp fresh garlic, pressed or finely
   chopped
1 cup Cheddar cheese, shredded
½ cup Preston Chardonnay

Preheat oven to 350°.

Remove stems from mushrooms – discard. Hollow out inside of mushrooms (a grapefruit spoon works great); saving the meat and setting aside in a bowl. Set mushroom caps in a baking dish.

Melt butter and garlic in a medium skillet. Add wine, onions, mushroom meat and celery. Cook until tender. Remove from heat and add ½ cup of shredded cheese – stir well. Stuff mushrooms with mixture and sprinkle with remaining cheese.

Bake in oven 10 minutes or until mushrooms are tender.

Sausage and Cheese Appetizers

▼▼

Makes 75

3 cups Bisquick mix

24 oz Jimmy Dean Hot Sausage,
  uncooked

4 cups Cheddar cheese, grated

3 Tbsp green onions, chopped

¼ cup cold Preston Pinot Noir
  Blanc

Let cheese soften at room temperature and add remaining
ingredients. Roll in walnut-size balls. Bake in 400° preheated
oven for 20 minutes or until golden brown. Best served warm.

Bill's Special Filet Mignon

▼▼▼

Serves 4

2½ lb filet mignon (roast)
1 tsp Worcestershire sauce
fresh garlic
lemon

salt and pepper
½ cup Preston Cabernet
  Sauvignon

Poke 5 or 6 holes in roast and fill with whole peppercorns. Marinate roast in wine and Worcestershire sauce for 1 hour, then rub roast with fresh garlic, lemon, pepper and salt.

Put roast on rotisserie spit and cook over medium heat for 10 to 15 minutes to sear, then turn to low heat and cook for 1 hour, over 4 pieces of Cabernet Wood Chips (soaked in water).

Slice into 4 10-oz steaks or chill overnight and slice thin for delicious hors d'oeuvres.

RAIN CITY GRILL

2359 10th Ave East
Seattle, Washington 98102
(206) 325-5003

Decorated with over 100 multi-colored bumbershoots, Rain City Grill is Seattle's reigning Northwest restaurant. Featuring the freshest local seafood, meats, and produce to create exciting and flavorful dishes, Chef Diana Dillard (married to owner Tom Dillard two weeks before the Bite) is always on the lookout for fun new items to add to the menu.

While emphasis is on seafood, the menu is well balanced with offerings such as pork tenderloin with spicy peanut sauce, veal and porcini raviolis in a spinach fennel cream, and roast Oregon duckling with port sauce.

The atmosphere in the dining room is not stuffy or pretentious. Guests are encouraged to relax and take advantage of crayons and paper tableclothes while looking over an excellent wine list or having a cocktail. The Seattle P.I. said it best in their 3½-star review..."great sauces, service was tops, a good value."

Pork Tenderloin with Spicy Peanut Sauce

▼▼

Serves 6

½ cup creamy peanut butter
½ oz red curry paste*
1 oz rice wine vinegar
½ tsp minced garlic
1 Tbsp honey

¼ oz soy sauce
3 lbs pork tenderloin
    (approx 8 oz per person)
salt and pepper
chicken stock

Puree first 6 ingredients in a food processor (this is your base).

Season pork and sear on all sides. Finish in a 350° oven to desired doneness. We feel this dish is best at 135° in center.

While pork is in the oven, whisk together in a saucepan 1 oz peanut base per person to 2 ounces (¼ cup) of chicken stock. Reduce to desired consistency.

Pour sauce on plate. Slice pork and fan out on top of sauce. Garnish with roasted chopped peanuts and a small dice of red peppers.

*Red curry paste is available at Uwajimaya or most oriental groceries.

Lemon-Coconut Tart

▼▼

Serves 12

1 cup lemon juice
¾ cup granulated sugar
1 Tbsp cornstarch
6 egg yolks

1 cup cream (heat, cool)
1 shallow 10" partially baked
   pastry shell
1½ cups lightly toasted coconut

Whisk the egg yolks, cornstarch, and sugar together. With a spoon, stir in lemon juice and cream. Be careful not to create air bubbles. Carefully pour mixture into pastry shell.

Bake for 30–40 minutes or until done at 350°. Will be a little soft until completely cool.

Sprinkle with toasted coconut. Best served slightly warmed with a little whipped cream.

Spinach Salad with Orange-Sesame Dressing

Serves 12

Dressing:
¼ cup rice wine vinegar
¾ cup salad oil
1 Tbsp sesame oil
1 tsp fresh chopped garlic
¼ cup orange juice
2 tsp wasabi powder*
   (or 1 tsp dry mustard)

2 Tbsp honey
dash salt
thoroughly cleaned spinach
Garnish:
chopped toasted hazelnuts
orange segments

Mix first 8 ingredients together thoroughly. Heat ⅛ cup dressing per small salad (spinach). Pour over spinach in mixing bowl. Toss and put on plate.

Garnish with orange segments, toasted, chopped hazelnuts and a small slice of red pepper.

*Wasabi powder is available at Uwajimaya or most Asian groceries. Similar to horseradish, the root is dried and pulverized. Mixed with water to form a paste and frequently used with sashimi.

Ristorante Paparazzi

2202 North 45th
Seattle, Washington 98103
(206) 547-7772

Calamari Fritti with Aioli Sauce

Serves 4

1 lb fresh, whole sm calamari
½ cup flour
2 cups extra virgin olive oil
Aoli sauce:
2 eggs (one separated)
¼ cup vegetable oil

1 oz fresh garlic
2 oz artichoke hearts
1 tsp dijon mustard
dash Worcestershire
pinch white pepper
vegetable stock

Saute artichoke hearts in a small amount of vegetable stock for five minutes until tender. Drain and set aside.

Place the following in a Cuisinart or similar food processor: one whole egg, the yolk of the second egg, dijon mustard, and white pepper. Start mixing with the Cuisinart, adding vegetable oil slowly (if oil is added too fast the mixture may break up).

Add drained artichokes to mixture along with fresh garlic and Worcestershire. Continue mixing until pureed and smooth.

Prepare calamari by removing skin and fins as well as all internal matter, retaining the tentacles. Rinse well and drain on paper towels. Lay calamari tubes on a flat surface and cut into ¼" rings.

Preheat olive oil to 325° in small fryer or similar cooking environment. Dredge calamari in flour lightly, being sure to shake off any excess. Submerge calamari rings in preheated oil, being careful not to overcrowd, for approximately two minutes. Remove and drain on paper towels. Serve with fresh lemon, water cress garnish and aoli on the side.

Roasted Red Pepper Soup

▼▼▼

Makes about 5 quarts

12 red bell peppers	salt
2 med white or yellow onions	pepper
¼ lb butter	12 oz tomatoes, diced
½ tsp curry	8 cups vegetable stock
½ cup flour	1 cup cream
1 tsp Worcestershire sauce	

Roast, seed and peel one dozen red bell peppers (if you are unfamiliar with this process there are canned products available).*

Start by making a fresh vegetable stock. You will need approximately ½ gallon, strained. Bring vegetable stock to simmer in a large soup pot. Puree bell peppers along with tomatoes in a food processor. Add to stock.

Puree onions and garlic. Melt butter in large saute skillet; add onions and garlic. Saute until translucent. Stir flour and curry into mixture.

Bring stock mixture to a very slow boil, then reduce heat to a simmer, adding flour mixture slowly until soup begins to thicken. Be careful to use only as much as is needed. Add salt, pepper, Worcestershire sauce, and cream. Stir and heat through.

*Place peppers under broiler until skins blister. Remove from oven and place in paper bag till cooled. Skins should remove easily.

Veal Rolls Melenaise

▼▼▼

Serves 4

1 lb fresh provimi veal leg
1 lb fresh asparagus
1 bunch fresh sage
4 oz Gorgonzola cheese, crumbled
4 oz sliced prosciutto ham
1 cup flour

butter
Sauce:
4 Tbsp butter
8 oz marsala
½ cup brandy

Trim veal leg and slice thinly into two-ounce portions. Using a meat mallet, pound veal portions until approximately 3"x5" and paper thin.

Trim asparagus and steam for approximately two minutes. Lay prosciutto atop pounded veal portions. Place asparagus, diced sage and Gorgonzola crumbles lengthwise across prosciutto and roll, securing the ends.

Dredge veal rolls in flour, shake off all excess. Saute in butter on medium low heat (being careful not to scorch the butter) until lightly browned. Bake in 350° oven for eight minutes while preparing sauce.

For the sauce: melt butter in a medium saute skillet. Add the brandy and marsala burning off all alcohol content. Reduce sauce to a thick caramel consistency. Serve atop veal and garnish appropriately.

114

CHICKEN AND RIBS

Award Winning B-B-Q

401 Broadway East
Seattle, Washington 98109
(206) 443-0728

To the Staff and Management
of Hickory Chicken & Ribs:

Thank you for being so understanding and wonderful with all our last minute food orders during Bumbershoot. Your hot meals saved the day for us. Everyone enjoyed the food, including Smokey Robinson, Fats Domino, and Jerry Lee Lewis.

Again, thank you. If we're around next year we will be looking forward to doing business with you.

Maxine Chen
Paul Gjefle
Caterers, Bumbershoot

Sizzlin' Dixie Country Pork Chops

▼▼

Serves 10

Sauce:
1 lb butter
1 Tbsp minced garlic
3 Tbsp minced parsley
1 Tbsp hot pepper sauce

Seasoning Mix:
1 envelope (7.6 oz) Italian
  dressing mix
2 Tbsp dry mustard
8 oz flour
20 pork chops
vegetable oil (as needed)

Melt butter in saucepan. Add garlic, parsley and pepper sauce. Brown for 2 minutes.

Combine salad dressing mix with dry mustard. Combine ½ cup of seasoning mixture with flour. Sprinkle pork chops with remaining seasoning mixture. Just before frying, dredge chops in seasoned flour.

Fry chops in ¼" deep hot oil until golden brown on each side, about 8–9 minutes each side.

Serve with sauce and barbequed baked beans.

FOUR⊕10

Fourth and Wall Street
Seattle, Washington 98121
(206) 728-0410

Holiday Magazine has consistently selected Rosellini's Four-10 Restaurant as one of America's award winning restaurants. The spirit behind this cheerful and elegant restaurant is that of Victor Rosellini, one of the nation's most amiable hosts. This elegant continental restaurant offers an exciting menu that utilizes many of the fine products unique to the Pacific Northwest. The wine list at the Four-10 cannot be overlooked, as it offers a fine selection of great wines both American and imported.

The experienced and knowledgeable staff at Rosellini's Four-10 are available to make your dining the most enjoyable ever. Rosellini's Four-10 is located within a few blocks of Seattle's better stores, theatres and office buildings. Come and enjoy a relaxing and elegant dining experience at one of Seattle's best restaurants.

Cappelletti with Meat & Tomato Sauce

Serves 4–6

1 sm onion	6 Tbsp dry red wine
1 sm stalk (rib) celery	2 cups peeled, diced tomatoes
1 sm carrot	1 cup stock (beef or veal)
1 clove garlic	salt and pepper, to taste
2 basil leaves	6 Tbsp cream
1 cup bacon, chopped	1 lb cappelletti or tortellini
¼ cup butter	parmesan cheese, grated
¼ cup ground beef or veal	

Chop onion, celery, carrot, garlic, basil, and bacon. Melt butter. Gently brown chopped vegetables and bacon with beef or veal, stirring gently, over low heat. Stir in stock or tomatoes. Season carefully with small amount of salt (bacon may be salty) and freshly ground black pepper.

Cook over low heat for approximately 30 minutes, stirring occasionally. Just before removing sauce from the heat, stir in cream.

Mix well with pasta and serve very hot. Serve grated parmesan cheese separately.

Cappelletti (or tortellini): Bring water to boil in 2 quart pan. Add salt. Add pasta slowly, stirring gently so pasta does not stick together. Cook approximately 12 to 15 minutes. Drain thoroughly. Add sauce and mix gently. Serve hot.

Veal Marsala

Serves 4

12 1½-oz pieces top round of veal, pounded thinly
¼ lb mushrooms, sliced
3 Tbsp olive oil
3 Tbsp butter

⅓ cup marsala
juice ½ lemon
flour for dredging
salt
black pepper

Dredge each piece of veal in flour. Season with salt and pepper. Heat oil over medium-high heat and brown veal on each side.

Drain oil from pan. Add butter and mushrooms. Saute veal and mushrooms 2-3 minutes. Add marsala and juice of ½ lemon (more if needed). Remove veal. Continue cooking sauce until slightly thickened.

Place veal on serving dish. Pour sauce over.

Semi-Freddo Torte

Makes 1 cake

1 sm package vanilla pudding
   mix, prepared with:

1 cup whipping cream

1 cup half and half

pound cake, loaf size, sliced
   horizontally into 3 layers

½ to 1 lb semi-sweet chocolate,
   finely chopped

½ cup rum

½ cup brandy

1 cup anisette

Place first layer of cake on serving plate. Soak with one third of the liquor mix (rum, brandy and anisette). Mix chopped chocolate with pudding, spread on cake in a layer about ½" thick. Repeat layers of pound cake, liquor and pudding mix. Sprinkle top with mix of powdered sugar and cocoa. Refrigerate at least four hours.

THE RUSTY PELICAN

1111 Fairview Ave North
Seattle, Washington 98109
(206) 622-0200

The Rusty Pelican, located on scenic Lake Union, offers a wide variety of fresh, local and exotic seafoods. Choose from award-winners such as fresh swordfish malia or fresh halibut with a spicy orange-ginger glaze.

Experience the romantic atmsphere, see one of the best views on Lake Union, and taste why our food was chosen "Best Entree" for two consecutive years at the Bite of Seattle.

Enjoy live entertainment six nights a week in our lounge and complimentary valet parking.

Fresh Swordfish with Oriental Glaze

▼▼▼

Serves 4

Marinade (yields 1½ qts):
4 oz fresh ginger
2 Tbsp fresh garlic
2 cup Hoisin sauce
1 cup chile garlic paste

6 oz brown sugar
1 cup soy sauce
½ cup honey
1½ cups water
4 fresh swordfish steaks

Peel and grate ginger root. Mince to puree with sharp knife. Peel garlic and mince. Combine ginger, garlic and remaining ingredients (except swordfish steaks) into large mixing bowl and mix with wire whip.

Refrigerate for 12 hours before using.

Marinate swordfish steaks for one hour. Charbroil swordfish, basting with marinade.

Stuart Anderson's

9 Seattle locations: Lynnwood, Renton, Burien, Lakewood, Bellevue (Crossroads), Federal Way, Bremerton, Bellingham and Everett.

Stuart Anderson's Black Angus Restaurant opened in Seattle, Washington on April 1, 1964. The original formula included a complete steak dinner at a reasonable price, friendly service and comfortable surroundings. This formula has changed only slightly over the years to allow more menu diversity in response to changing cutomer tastes. The first restaurant was very successful and ten additional locations were opened in the first eight years.

In 1984, the chain became the largest steak dinner-house chain in market share nationwide. We believe this is because of our dedica- tion to quality service for our customers.

Stuart Anderson's Restaurants now serve customers in 18 states and feature not only the finest quality beef, but delicious fresh fish and grilled chicken specialties.

Beef Kabobs with Sesame Sauce

▼▼▼

Serves 4

1 lb New York tenderloin, cut into 1" cubes

1 lb top sirloin, cut into 1" cubes

1" cubes green pepper

1" cubes red pepper

1" wedge onion

12" wooden skewers

Marinade:

¼ cup salad oil

¼ cup sesame oil

Sesame sauce:

¼ cup sesame seeds

2 cups soy sauce

10 oz white sugar

2 tsp crushed red chili pepper

2 tsp black pepper

1 oz garlic, fresh, minced

½ oz ginger, fresh, shredded

Combine salad oil and sesame oil. Marinate beef in mixture 24 hours.

Toast sesame seeds. Combine sesame sauce ingredients. Mix very well to dissolve sugar.

Soak skewers in water. Skewer kabobs in the following order: beef, green pepper, beef, red pepper, beef, onion, beef. Brush with sesame sauce and broil over open flame or coals.

The Stuffed Shirt Catering Company

Waikiki Luau
6045 California Avenue SW
Seattle, Washington 98136
(206) 938-8551

Waikiki Luau was created by David and Marilyn Alefaio, the owners of the Stuffed Shirt Catering Company, as a festival food theme. This theme was chosen to reflect their Polynesian heritage. Many years ago they began their business caterings luaus for organizations all over Western Washington. The Stuffed Shirt Catering Company offers a large variety of interesting and well-prepared foods at very reasonable prices. Service ranges from breakfast or lunch for small business meetings to large parties and receptions. Their West Seattle store is open Monday through Saturday from 9:00 am until 6:30 pm with deli and bakery takeout available.

Bourbon and Macadamia Nut Cake

Makes 1 cake

1 Duncan Hines yellow cake mix
   with pudding
½ cup oil
½ cup water
4 eggs
½ cup bourbon or whiskey
½ cup macadamia nuts

Glaze:
1 cup sugar
½ cup butter
¼ cup water
¼ tsp lemon extract
1 tsp bourbon (optional)

Mix the first five ingredients until well blended. Grease the inside of a Bundt pan and sprinkle the nuts over the bottom of the pan. Pour batter into the pan and bake at 325° for 45 minutes.

Boil all of the glaze ingredients in a saucepan for three minutes. While cake is still hot, poke holes in it with a bamboo skewer and pour glaze over the cake.

Cool cake in the pan. When it is cool, invert pan on a serving dish to remove the cake. Sprinkle the cake with powdered sugar.

Party Fruit Basket

▼▼

Serves 25-35

1 pineapple

1 sm canteloupe

1 sm honeydew melon

2 lbs seedless grapes, cut in small clusters

2 pints strawberries

1 head of green leaf lettuce

Fruit salad dressing:

1 6-oz can lemonade

⅓ cup sugar

2 beaten eggs

½ pint whipping cream

To prepare dressing: mix the lemonade, sugar and eggs and cook over simmering water until thickened. Cool. Beat whipping cream and fold into lemonade mixture.

To prepare fruit basket: line a large basket with plastic wrap and then the washed leaf lettuce. Cut pineapple into quarters, then run a grapefruit knife between the skin and flesh of pineapple to loosen. Cut pineapple meat into ½" wedges and replace on the skin of the fruit. Arrange the four quarters in basket. Cut melon into wedges and place in basket.

Add little grape clusters and berries for garnish, leaving a space in center for a hollowed-out orange or grapefruit. Fill the orange with the dressing.

Oriental Spinach Salad

▼▼

Serves 2-4

1 lb spinach, torn into bite-sized
   pieces
1½ cups bean sprouts
1 cup sliced raw mushrooms
¼ cup toasted sunflower seeds
¼ cup sliced water chestnuts

⅔ cup oil
¼ cup soy sauce
2 Tbsp lemon juice
1½ tsp finely chopped green onion
½ tsp sugar
½ tsp pepper

Combine all ingredients in the second column and shake together in a jar.

Prepare salad, and just before serving toss with the dressing.

Sun Mountain Lodge

Presented by

Village Resorts, Inc.

A Collection Of Fine Resorts

P.O. Box 1000
Patterson Lake Road
Winthrop, Washington 98862
(509) 996-2211

Set with a commanding view of the Methow Valley, Sun Mountain Lodge Restaurant is highly acclaimed for its sophisticated regional cuisine. Featuring in-house smoked meats and game products.

Executive Chef Jack Haynes' portfolio includes a tenure at Salishan Resort in Oregon and Sun Rise Springs Health Resort in New Mexico.

These experiences coupled with his Japanese heritage have served to make Sun Mountain Lodge Restaurant an experience to come back to.

Spicy Sauteed Shrimp Appetizer

▼▼

Serves 4

25 shrimp (21/25 count per lb)

2 oz olive oil

1 tsp garlic

3 oz white wine

¾ oz lemon juice

3 oz oyster mushrooms

¼ cup diced green onions

¼ tsp cayenne pepper

½ tsp paprika

⅛ tsp black pepper

4 oz heavy cream

2½ Tbsp sweet butter

4 green pepper bottoms, 1" high

salt to taste

1 lemon cut into quarters, then sliced to make fan

In a large skillet, saute shrimp in olive oil, add garlic, mushrooms, then de-glaze pan with white wine and reduce. Next, add seasoning and heavy cream, reduce. Add tomatoes and green onions, simmer, remove from heat and fold in butter slowly. Salt to taste.

Broil pepper bottoms and use as bowls to place shrimp into. Pour sauce over shrimp and garnish with lemon fan and a sprig of dill.

Smoked Duck with Plum Sauce

▼▼▼

Serves 6–8

two ducks, 4 to 5 lbs
1 red apple, diced
1 white onion, diced
¼ cup salted black beans*
1 tsp star anise*
1 tsp chopped ginger
1 tsp chopped garlic
1 stick cinnamon
¼ cup soy sauce
½ tsp whole cloves
4 bay leaves
1 tsp black peppercorns

Sauce:
1 cup duck stock
¼ cup red wine
2 oz brandy
8 fresh plums
½ cup sugar
⅛ cup orange juice
1 oz lemon juice
1 stick cinnamon
1 star anise*
1½ tsp fresh chopped ginger
hickory & apple wood chips
two bamboo skewers

Mix ingredients in column one (except ducks) in large bowl.

Prep ducks by removing excess fat, wings to first joint, and to knuckle on thigh. Then fill cavity with the mixture and sew skin together by tightly pulling shut with bamboo skewers. Smoke over wood chips in covered barbeque for 2 hours, then finish in 350° oven until meat is 160 degrees internally. Let cool and bone carefully, leaving skin on meat.

Prepare stock by using excess bones and ½ diced onion. Cover with water and simmer ½ hour. Strain.

For sauce: in separate pan carmelize sugar, add red wine, lemon juice and orange juice. Season with 1 stick cinnamon and 1 star anise. Finish base sauce by adding 1 cup stock and 4 plums, halved and pitted. Season with 1 tsp chopped ginger. Simmer 20 minutes; then strain. Return to heat and thicken with cornstarch.

continued on the following page

Finish duck by sauteing in ½ oz oil, skin side down, then flip over and place in 425° oven for 12 to 15 minutes. Skin should be crisp. Remove excess oil from pan and saute ½ tsp of ginger and deglaze with 2 oz brandy. Simmer 4 plums, pitted, halved, and sliced into fans. Add to the sauce.

Serve duck with sauce placed on bottom and fanned plum on top for garnish.

*Available in Asian markets.

"TCBY"

The Country's Best Yogurt ®

Locations include Woodinville, Bellevue, Seattle, Kent, Tacoma, Puyallup, Mill Creek, Everett, Lynnwood (T.J. Maxx Plaza), Lynnwood (Mukilteo Speedway), Marysville, and Silverdale

TCBY frozen yogurt is a delicious, creamy, 96% fat free treat by itself, with only about half the calories of premium ice cream! Now you can enjoy it three new ways that are sure to please your palate.

Cocoa Raspberry Cake

▼▼▼

Serves 12 – 16

1¼ cups plus ⅓ cup TCBY
  Frozen Raspberry Yogurt
2⅓ cups all-purpose flour
⅔ cup unsweetened cocoa powder
1 tsp salt
½ tsp baking powder

¼ tsp baking soda
1½ cups butter or margarine,
  softened
3 cups granulated sugar
2 tsp vanilla
1½ cups confectioners sugar, sifted

Thaw yogurt in refrigerator overnight. (Keep thawed yogurt refrigerated. Like all dairy products, yogurt should not be left at room temperature for an extended period of time or it will spoil. It is recommended that thawed yogurt be used within 2 to 3 days. If normal separation occurs during thawing, shake or mix before using.)

Preheat oven to 325°. Grease and flour 12-cup Bundt pan or 10" tube pan and set aside.

Sift flour, cocoa, salt, baking powder and baking soda. Beat butter and granulated sugar in large bowl until light and fluffy. Add eggs, one at a time, beating well after each addition.

Add flour-cocoa mixture to butter mixture alternately with 1¼ cups yogurt and beat until blended (refrigerate remaining ⅓ cup yogurt until ready to use).

Pour batter into prepared pan and smooth top. Bake one hour plus 10 – 20 minutes, or until cake tester inserted in center of cake comes out clean.

Cool in pan on wire rack 15 minutes. Remove from pan and cool completely on rack. Place reserved ⅓ cup yogurt in small bowl, add confectioners sugar and beat vigorously with wire whisk until smooth. Refrigerate 45 minutes.

Stir glaze well and spoon or drizzle over top of cooled cake. Refrigerate until ready to serve.

Pina Colada Punch

▼▼▼

Makes 38 4-oz servings

1 bottle (2 liters) chilled ginger ale
1 bottle (2 liters) chilled lemon-
lime flavored soda or
carbonated water

1 container (27 oz) TCBY Frozen
Aloe Pina Colada Yogurt
frozen pineapple rings
sliced kiwi fruit
fresh fruit slices to decorate

Pour ginger ale and soda into large punch bowl. Add frozen yogurt by large spoonfuls. Stir a few times.

To decorate, float fruit on top of punch. Ladle into punch cups.

Variations: substitute Aloe Tropical Fruit Yogurt, Eggnog Yogurt or your favorite Frozen Fruit Yogurt for Aloe Pina Colada Yogurt.

Calories per 4-oz serving: 65.

Summer Fruit Salad with Mango Dressing

2 cups honeydew melon or
    canteloupe balls

2 nectarines or peaches, peeled,
    pitted and sliced

1 cup green or red seedless grapes,
    cut in half

1 cup blueberries

1 cup sliced strawberries

Boston lettuce

Mango dressing:

¾ cup TCBY Frozen Tango
    Mango Yogurt

½ cup light mayonnaise

1 Tbsp honey

1 Tbsp cider vinegar

½ tsp grated orange peel

Combine melon balls, nectarines, grapes, blueberries and strawberries in medium-sized bowl. Line salad plate with lettuce leaves. Spoon fruit mixture onto center of lettuce and refrigerate until ready to serve.

Set yogurt aside at room temperature 15 minutes before serving time to soften slightly. Stir mayonnaise, honey, vinegar and orange peel in bowl with wire whisk until blended. Stir in yogurt. Spoon over fruit and serve immediately.

Calories per serving of salad (6th of recipe): 145. Mango dressing: 25 calories per Tbsp.

"HASTA PUEDES TOMAR EL AGUA"

TLAQUEPAQUE Bar

1122 Post Avenue
Seattle, Washington 98101
(206) 467-8226

The Tlaquepaque Bar originated with the concept of authentic gourmet Mexican cuisine and genuine Mexican hospitality. Specializing in regional dishes, the restaurant shies away from the typical rice and bean house menu.

Patrons of the Tlaquepaque Bar will attest to the fact that ambience plays a major role in the restaurant's appeal. When you walk through the front doors you walk into Mexico! Bright lights, happy people and a friendly staff make the fine food and good times even more memorable.

Tlaquepaque Bar Guacamole

▼▼

Serves 10-12

10 avocados, skinned and stoned

1 bunch cilantro, chopped fine

1 tomato, diced

1 Tbsp garlic salt

½ cup lime juice

1 cup green onion, chopped

Smash avocado velvety smooth by adding the lime juice while using a potato masher. Add the garlic salt, green onion, and cilantro. Mix well with a large wooden spoon. Fold in the diced tomatoes.

Don't try adding sour cream, mayonnaise, or anything else someone might suggest! These are good ways to S-T-R-E-T-C-H your guacamole, but it will also ruin the quality.

Serve with fresh fried chips, salsa, and a cold one!

Fajitas al Mesquite

Serves 2–10

3 lbs unpeeled outside skirt steak
10 whole limes
1 Tbsp garlic salt
1 tsp black pepper

mesquite wood
mesquite charcoal
1 match

Trim skin off of skirt steak and butterfly until paper thin, and cut into thin strips. Cover generously with lime juice, garlic salt, and black pepper. Let marinate overnight.

Broil over mesquite coals. Serve in a hot flour tortilla with hot sauce and pico de gallo relish.

For pico de gallo relish: combine equal amounts of chopped serrano peppers, anaheim peppers, tomato, onion, lime juice, and spices.

Recipe serves 2 to 10 people, depending on how much tequila they have consumed!

Camarones Tocino

Serves 2

6 bacon strips

12 large prawns

4 whole pickled jalapenos,
  quartered lengthwise

batter for deep frying (beer batter
  or your favorite recipe will do)

Split prawns. Stuff with a thin slice of jalapeno and wrap with ½ slice baon. Put prawns on bamboo skewer (3 to skewer), dip in a beer batter and deep fry.

After frying, baste prawns with a jalapeno and cilantro vinegar sweet and sour sauce. Serve on a bed of rice with a pineapple wedge garnish.

White Heron Cellars

PO Box 5245
102 Chinook
George, Washington 98824
(509) 785-5521

White Heron Cellars is owned by Phyllis and Cameron Fries and produces a Dry Johannisberg Riesling and a Pinot Noir, currently available throughout Washington State and Colorado. White Heron Cellars produces quality wines at moderate prices.

The winery is located in George, Washington. Land has been acquired at Trinidad, a ghost town between Quincy and Wenatchee, overlooking the Columbia River and Crescent Bar Resort. Grapes will be planted in the spring of 1990 and by the turn of the century White Heron Cellars will produce Syrah, a Bordeaux style blend (the 1988 Cabernet/Merlot blend is aging nicely in barrels), Pinot Noir, Dry Johannisberg Riesling, and Rousanne.

Cameron has been working in the Washington wine industry since the 1984 harvest. As head winemaker at Worden's Winery in Spokane, he won numerous medals. In 1986 he moved to Champs de Brionne winery where he is currently head winemaker.

The White Heron wines reflect a central European style of winemaking. Phyllis and Cameron spent five years in Switzerland, where Cameron attended L'ecole superieur d'oenologie et de viticulture de Changins in Nyon. He worked as an apprentice with various vineyards of the Lavaux region.

Swiss French Wine Pie

▼▼

Serves 6–8

1 Tbsp cornstarch

3 Tbsp sugar

1¼ cup dry White Heron Riesling

1 baked 9" pie shell

Mix cornstarch and sugar in a bowl. Add wine, mix well. Add mixture to baked pie shell. Bake 20 to 25 minutes at 425°. Filling will be a clear gel when you remove from oven. Cool three to four hours.

Yakima River

Route 1 Box 1657
North River Road
Prosser, Washington 99350
(509) 786-2805

A family-owned and operated winery, we are professionals who take pride in our work. Winemaker – John Rauner. Yakima River Winery is large enough to ensure reliability and consistency of supply, yet not so large as to have lost the personal touch in its operation.

We specialize in oak aged red wines and special dessert wines. Open for tastings every day. Hours are from 10:00 am to 5:00 pm.

Large tours need to call in advance.

Rauner Family BBQ Sauce & Ribs

▼▼▼

Makes approximately 3 cups

16 oz bottle soy sauce
2 Tbsp basil
3 Tbsp rosemary
4 Tbsp granulated sugar
2 Tbsp dry mustard
2 Tbsp salt

2 sm minced Walla Walla sweet onion
2 Tbsp olive oil
6 oz Yakima River Merlot
1 Tbsp ground fresh pepper
beef or pork ribs

Place ingredients in sauce pan and simmer a few minutes. Let cool.

Place the ribs in a large pan and cover with the sauce. Cover pan with foil and bake at 350° until done.

Reduced Wine Sauce

Makes approximately 1 cup

2 cups Yakima River Cabernet
1 Tbsp tomato paste
2-3 beef or chicken bouillon cubes

pinch of nutmeg
¼ lb unsalted butter, cut into 1"cubes

Let the wine simmer on low heat (uncovered) until reduced by half. Add remaining ingredients, excluding butter, and simmer a while longer.

Bring wine to near boiling and whisk in butter, one piece at a time, until sauce is smooth, thick and "glossy."

Excellent with wild game, pork, lamb and duck.

Hinterberger's Alley

- The Beeliner Diner • Café Juanita
- Chinook's at Salmon Bay
- Cucina! Cucina! • Ezell's Fried Chicken
- Fuller's • Green Lake Grill
- Landau's • Las Margaritas
- Rover's Restaurant

A benefit for Northwest Harvest sponsored by

The Seattle Times

John Hinterberger's
Skillet Spaghetti Sauce

▼▼

This recipe and the method for preparing it date back to my college years at the University of Connecticut. As an Army veteran and after three years in airborne units, I found living in a college dormitory a little restricted and fraternity life more than a little silly.

I moved off campus to a small cabin on a nearby lake and, with a variety of roommates over the semesters, set up housekeeping. There were dozens, perhaps hundreds, of other vets doing the same thing – going to school on $110 a month of G.I. Bill allotments.

It wasn't easy. But it was possible. One of the problems was food. We cabin dwellers didn't, of course, have dormitory food privileges. Restaurants were out of the question. But we liked to eat, some of use liked to eat well, and on weekends we liked to party.

I came up with this recipe as a means of entertaining on the cheap. Ingredient amounts could be adjusted to fit the number of folks coming over for the evening. And the leftover sauce could always be used over a meatloaf, or form the basis for an Italian-accented pot roast later in the week.

Preparation centered on the use of a large (12-inch), black, well-seasoned cast-iron skillet, a cooking utensil I became so attached to, that I hand-carried it to Mexico the year I graduated, and carted it a few thousand more miles northwest when I enrolled at the University of Washington for graduate school. I still have it.

If you don't have one, get one. They are cheap, cook well and will last longer than you will.

½ cup plus 1 Tbsp olive oil	1 6-oz can tomato paste
1 lg onion	1 28-oz can tomato puree
1 med carrot	1 28-oz can Italian plum tomatoes
salt and pepper	1 cup dry red wine
4-6 large cloves garlic	1 lb spaghetti
1 tsp sugar	freshly grated parmesan or
2 Tbsp fresh basil	Romano cheese
1 bay leaf	
2 Tbsp fresh oregano	

continued on following page

149

In a well-seasoned (or heavily oiled) cast-iron skillet, slowly heat one-half cup good quality olive oil. Mince onion and carrot. Place both on a cutting board and mince further with one or two chef's knives until you have created a rather coarse paste. (Note: this does not work well in a blender or food processor, which tend to over-blend and aerate the vegetables into a mousse.)

The finished product in Italian is called a *battuto*. Add it to the olive oil, which should not be hot enough to brown the mixture. Cook slowly with salt and pepper to taste for 10 minutes until the battuto has very slightly colored. Add four to six cloves of minced garlic and one teaspoon of sugar. Continue to simmer another 10 minutes until most of the moisture in the onion-carrot mix has been driven off, but neither the *battuto* nor garlic has browned.

The sauce may be made without carrot, but if not, increase the amount of sugar to two teaspoons.

At this point I add a combination of basil (preferably fresh, but dried will do), a bay leaf and oregano. Over the years I have varied the amounts of these and you can, too. But about two Tbsp each of basil and oregano will do. Use a quality Italian or Greek oregano. Some brands available on market shelves can be more bitter than fragrant. Sniff first.

Now add tomato paste. Stir until the paste heats and takes on an oily sheen. Add tomato puree (be choosy about the brand) and Italian plum tomatoes (which you have chopped) along with the can juices. Look for imported canned tomatoes in Italian specialty stores, or some very good domestic packs from Texas and San Jose.

Pour in one cup of a good, dry red wine. Stir. Place a glass cover over the skillet, leaving a gap to let steam escape and simmer over very slow heat for at least two hours.

This recipe can be made with garden fresh tomatoes (6 to 8 cups chopped and seeded). I leave the peels on. I like them. But do not try to make the sauce using pale, half-ripe grocery-store tomatoes. They seldom have enough flavor.

When the sauce is done, spoon most of it into a serving bowl, leaving a quarter- to half-inch layer in the bottom of the skillet. Add one Tbsp olive oil and heat.

Cook a pound or more of spaghetti to package directions, firm but not crunchy. Drain well, but do not rinse. Add it to the sauce in the skillet and toss over medium-low heat for one minute until all of the pasta is lightly coated with the oily sauce. Don't ask why. Just do it.

You can now pour the spaghetti onto a large serving platter, dust generously with freshly-grated Parmesan or Romano cheese and an added layer of sauce and Parmesan down the middle of the pasta. At my place, however, the spaghetti was always brought to the table sizzling in the skillet. Serves a bunch.

A loaf of bread. A cup of wine. Wow.

Beeliner Diner

2114 North 45th Street
Seattle, Washington
(206) 547-6313

The Beeliner Diner in beautiful downtown Wallingford takes you back to an era of high quality, simply prepared foods.

Opened in answer to overpriced "Northwest" restaurants and a proliferation of ethnic dining spots in the Seattle area, the diner serves ample portions of basic American food.

Try the turkey pot pie, charcoal grilled pork chops or a roast chicken. Sandwich offerings include the Hiway Hamburger, chili dogs or a Market House Reuben.

So get in here and pull up a counter stool!

Here's a hearty beef stew recipe that we offer for our Monday blue plate special. Recommended primarily for a blustery fall or winter day, the recipe works just as well in the summertime here in the great Northwest.

Hearty Beef Stew

▼▼▼

Serves 5–6

1 cup salad oil
1 cup flour
2½ lbs stew meat
3 ribs of celery, cut into 1" pieces
1 quart peeled whole tomatoes
½ cup dry red wine
2 cups of rich beef stock
¼ cup tomato paste
2 bay leaves
1½ tsp whole thyme

1 tsp marjoram
2 tsp basil
salt & pepper to taste
3 cloves fresh minced garlic
1 lb boiling onions
1 lb carrots, peeled, cut in 1" pieces
¼ lb mushrooms
12 new potatoes, parboiled & halved

The preparation takes a little over two hours from start to finish, so start a fire in the fireplace, put on an Ella Fitzgerald album or two and enjoy.

In a small saucepan, heat salad oil. Stir in flour and cook over medium heat stirring constantly until you have a nut brown roux. Set aside.

Heat a six quart saucepan with deep sides very hot. Add the olive oil and brown stew meat. Sprinkle with fresh ground pepper.

Add ingredients listed from celery through garlic and bring to a boil. Introduce enough of the roux to thicken. Reduce heat and simmer for 30 minutes.

Add peeled whole boiling onions and simmer for additional 30 minutes. Add carrots and simmer for 30 minutes. Add mushrooms and parboiled new potatoes and simmer for at least 45 minutes, until stew meat is tender. Adjust seasonings to taste.

152

Fisherman's Terminal
1735 West Thurman
Seattle, Washington
(206) 283-4665

Chinook's offers unique waterfront dining, featuring fresh Northwest seafood at Fisherman's Terminal, home of the Washington and Alaska fishing fleets. The best of each season including such specialties as fresh Alaska halibut, prized Copper and Yukon River salmon, Dungeness crab, Northwest oysters, clams, mussels and singing scallops are offered in both traditional and bold, new preparations. Fisherman's breakfast is served Saturday and Sunday. Outside deck for warm weather dining. For casual dining, visit "Little Chinooks." Enjoy fish'n chips at the Terminal or have them wrapped to go.

Fresh Halibut
with Sour Cream, Red Onion & Fresh Dill

▼▼▼

Serves 4

4 7-8 oz fresh filets

8 oz dry white wine (Chardonnay)

1 tsp Kosher salt

1 cup fine, dry bread crumbs

1 cup mayonnaise

½ cup sour cream

½ cup red onion, very finely chopped

2 tsp fresh dill, chopped

4 sprigs fresh dill

Marinate the filets in white wine mixed with Kosher salt for 1 hour. Drain and coat each filet with bread crumbs. Mix mayonnaise, sour cream, red onion and fresh dill together. Spread on top of filets like frosting.

Place filets in baking dish moistened with 1 oz of white wine and 1 oz of water. Bake at 350° for approximately 8 minutes. Garnish with dill sprigs.

Almond Chicken Salad

Serves 4

3 heads Romaine, trimmed and julienne cut

1 lb boned breast of chicken, stir fried

Almond noodle mixture:

2 packages Top Ramen noodles, broken (season packet is not used)

6 oz blanched, slivered almonds

2 oz butter or margarine

Sesame dressing:

4 oz unseasoned rice vinegar

4 oz salad oil

3 Tbsp sugar

2 Tbsp soy sauce

2 Tbsp sesame oil

For almond noodle mixture: quickly stir fry noodles and almonds in butter. Cook until golden. Remove from heat and cool completely.

For sesame dressing: combine all ingredients in a bowl and whisk until blended.

To prepare: cut boned chicken breasts into ¼" slices. Quickly stir fry in soy sauce, butter or margarine and white wine. Remove from heat and cool completely.

Trim heads of Romaine. Cut heads horizontally in thin strips (¼" wide). Soak in 70° water. Spin dry and refrigerate.

Toss all ingredients in a large salad bowl. Top each serving with toasted sesame seeds and thinly sliced green onions. Garnish with pineapple wedges. Serve immediately.

901 Fairview Avenue North
Seattle, Washington
(206) 44-PASTA

17770 Southcenter Parkway
Tukwila, Washington
(206) 575-0520

A fun, lively gathering place featuring affordable Italian food (both "cutting edge" as well as traditional styles) in an attractive waterfront cafe on Lake Union in Seattle and in the busy retail shopping district of Parkway Plaza in Tukwila.

Linguine with Oven Roasted Chicken

Serves 1

1 oz olive oil

1 Tbsp roasted garlic puree

3 oz roasted chicken

1 tsp salt & pepper

1 Tbsp balsamic vinegar

2 oz chicken stock

4 oz reduced cream

3 oz blanched broccoli

1 oz whole butter

1½ oz goat cheese

¼ lb fresh linguine

Saute garlic, chicken, salt, and pepper in oil until chicken begins to color. Add vinegar and deglaze pan. Then add stock and reduce. Add cream and reduce until sauce begins to thicken slightly.

Cook linguine while sauce cooks. Drain pasta.

Add broccoli and butter to sauce and finish reducing. Add goat cheese and cooked pasta and combine with sauce.

Chop Chop Salad

▼▼▼

Serves 1

6 oz iceberg lettuce

2 oz diced tomato

1 oz chick peas

¼ oz fresh basil

1 oz mozzarella cheese

3 oz poached chicken

2 oz salami, julienned

½ oz provolone cheese, grated

Garnish:

½ oz scallions, chopped

1 oz tomato, chopped

Italian vinaigrette

Combine all the ingredients on a cutting board and chop until all items are of approximately the same size. Place chopped salad in mixing bowl and toss with dressing. Put on serving plate and garnish with diced tomatoes and scallions.

7850 Greenlake Drive North
Seattle, Washington 98103
(206) 522-3490

Roast Rabbit with Roasted Peppers

▼▼▼

Serves 2-4

4 saddle of rabbit (loin),
    bone removed
2 red peppers, roasted and peeled
1 head of garlic, peeled, the cloves
    left whole
1 cup dry vermouth

1½ cups rabbit or veal stock
¼ lb unsalted butter, cut into
    pieces
salt and pepper to taste
2 Tbsp olive oil

In a large saute pan brown the rabbit on both sides. Place in a small roasting pan and place in a 350° oven for 30 minutes. Place the garlic cloves in the saute pan and quickly brown. Deglaze the pan with the vermouth and bring to a boil. Add the stock and return to a boil. Reduce the liquid to ⅓ cup.

While the sauce is reducing, cut the peppers into ½" strips and add them to the sauce. Whip the butter into the sauce one piece at a time. Serve the sauce over the rabbit.

Tenderloin of Beef
with Red Wine, Walnuts & Oregon Blue Cheese Butter

▼▼

Makes approx. 1 lb compound butter

1 lb unsalted butter, cut in pieces
½ cup walnuts, finely chopped
2 cups red wine
1½ cups veal stock
4 sm tomatoes, chopped

2 bay leaves
1 Tbsp peppercorns
½ Tbsp thyme
2 Tbsp shallots, chopped
6-8 oz Oregon blue cheese
tenderloin steaks

Place wine, stock, tomato, herbs, pepper, and shallots in a saucepan and bring to a boil. Reduce by half and strain into another saucepan. Return to a boil and reduce to ¼ cup.

Place the butter, cheese and walnuts in a mixing bowl and begin to whip at low speed. Slowly add the reduced liquid to the butter while whipping. When the ingredients are incorporated roll the mixture into a log in wax paper.

Cook the steaks as you see fit. Top each one with a slice of the compound butter and serve.

Pagataw Pancakes

▼▼

Serves 6

⅓ cup flour
⅓ cup buttermilk
½ tsp lemon juice
2 egg yolks
salt and pepper
2 cups of cleaned corn

2 Tbsp red pepper, chopped and lightly sauteed
2 Tbsp chives, chopped
2 tsp cilantro, chopped
16 yearling oysters, chopped
6 egg whites, whipped to stiff peaks

Blend dry ingredients with milk, lemon juice and eggs until smooth. Mix in remaining ingredients except egg whites. Gently fold egg whites into pancake batter.

Cook as regular pancakes in hot peanut oil. The pancakes should be about 3½" in diameter.

Serve 2 pancakes per person. Top each pancake with a dollop of whipped cream with jalapeno pepper chopped and stirred in. Top the cream with a small dab of salmon roe.

Koll Center Bellevue, Ground Floor
500 108th Avenue NE
Bellevue, Washington 98004
(206) 646-6644

Landau's Restaurant serves a variety of Northwest favorites interspersed with dishes from the Pacific Rim. Since opening its doors in 1987, Landau's has been hailed as one of the best restaurants in the Pacific Northwest, receiving recognition both locally and nationally.

Awards and reviews include *Seattle Times* Top Ten Restaurant 1988; *Journal American* 4½ stars, highest rated restaurant; *Puget Sound Business Journal* "Everything is done with class, excellence and pride of presentation"; *Travel/Holiday Magazine* 1989 Fine Dining Award.

Located in Bellevue, with convenient complimentary valet parking, Landau's offers fine dining and attentive service in an atmosphere of comfortable elegance.

Black Bean Soup

▼▼

Serves 6 – 8

1 lb black beans
2 oz butter
2 lg onions, coarsely chopped
2 garlic cloves, crushed
1 celery stalk, finely chopped
6½ to 8 pints chicken stock
1½ lbs smoked ham hocks with
    bone and rind
2 bay leaves

2 cloves
8 peppercorns
salt
freshly ground black pepper
3 fl oz Madeira
Garnish:
2 hard boiled eggs
thin lemon slices

Soak the beans overnight in water to cover. Next day, drain beans. Melt butter in a large pot, add the onions, garlic, and celery and saute until vegetables become transparent, approximately 3 minutes. Carefully pour in the stock and stir.

Add the ham hocks, beans, bay leaves, cloves and peppercorns. Bring the stock to a boil, skim off the scum, reduce the heat and simmer. Partially cover the pot and let simmer this way for approximately 1½ hours, skimming soup as needed. Beans will be tender when soup is ready.

Remove soup from heat. Discard bones and rind. Put the soup through a food mill to puree the beans and vegetables.

Taste for seasoning. Add salt if needed (depends on saltiness of ham). Add pepper to taste.

Return soup to the pot, add the Madeira and bring to the boil. To serve: ladle soup into bowl. Float a thin slice of lemon on top with a grating of hard boiled egg.

Crabmeat Canneloni

Serves 4

Canneloni:

2 oz butter

5 shallots, minced

½ tsp Worcestershire Sauce

2 tsp Dijon mustard

1 lb Dungeness Crabmeat

8 crepes, use your favorite recipe
  or purchase ready made ones

1 cup Mornay Sauce (follows)

Mornay Sauce:

3 oz butter

3 oz flour

6 oz milk

4 oz cream

8 oz parmesan cheese, grated

For Mornay Sauce: in a saucepan, melt butter, add flour and stir to make a roux. Slowly, using a whisk, add milk and cream, whisking all the while to keep the sauce smooth. Bring to boil and stirring constantly, keep it at a boil for one minute. Take off the heat and stir in the cheese until it has melted.

For canneloni filling, melt butter in saute pan and add shallots. Saute until translucent. Add remaining ingredients and mix thoroughly until filling is hot.

To assemble: place ⅛ of filling in a crepe. Roll up and place in a buttered, oven tempered dish. Continue in this fashion with the rest of the crepes. Nap with Mornay Sauce and lightly sprinkle 2 Tbsp of Parmesan cheese over the top. Place under a broiler until sauce is lightly browned.

Serve with vegetables and/or a fresh garden salad.

Irish Coffee Mousse

▼▼▼

Serves 6

2 egg yolks
¼ cup granulated sugar
8 oz half and half
1 Tbsp gelatin
½ cup strong, hot, black coffee
2 Tbsp Irish Whiskey

2 egg whites at room temperature
¼ cup granulated sugar
⅔ cup whipping cream, whipped till it can hold peaks
3 oz semi-sweet chocolate, melted in microwave or over hot water

Put egg yolks and ¼ cup of sugar in mixing bowl and whip until it is light yellow in color and has thickened slightly. Heat half and half to near boil and whisk into the yolk mixture. Pour back into saucepan and over medium heat cook until the mixture coats the backs of a spoon. DO NOT BOIL. Stir continuously.

Add coffee to gelatin and stir to dissolve. Add this to the yolk mixture along with the Irish Whiskey. Refrigerate until cool.

Whip egg whites to soft peaks and gradually add ¼ cup of sugar. Fold into cooled yolk mixture. Pour into decorative glasses and chill in refrigerator until set, 2 to 4 hours.

Melt chocolate and pour a thin coating on top of each mousse. Rotate glass to cover it completely. Return to refrigerator until time to serve. When serving, pipe a rosette of whipped cream in the center of the mousse and add chocolate covered coffee bean and a sprig of mint for a final touch.

2808 East Madison
Seattle, Washington 98112
(206) 325-7442

Chef Thierry Rautureau and partner, pastry chef Diane Stein have owned Rover's since 1987. The restaurant is located on East Madison in a comfortable house which exudes a feeling of quiet sophistication and charm.

Chef Rautureau refers to the food he serves as "Northwest contemporary with a French accent." He uses local ingredients served with a touch of his homeland.

Rover's reputation is growing due to the imaginative and innovative style that features a changing menu and emphasizes the range of fresh and specialty foods available in the Northwest.

Lunch is served from 11:30 am to 2:00 pm; dinner is served from 5:30 pm to 9:00 pm.

Ratatouille
with Goat Cheese and Rosemary Sauce

▼▼

Serves 4

1 red onion, finely chopped
1 green zucchini, small dice
1 yellow zucchini, small dice
2 red bell peppers, small dice
½ eggplant, small dice
3 branches thyme, finely chopped
2 Tbsp olive oil
1 bunch basil, finely julienned

3 oz goat cheese, crumbled
Rosemary Sauce:
½ white onion, chopped
2 Tbsp butter
1 bunch rosemary
2 cups white wine
2 cups veal stock

For ratatouille: saute all ratatouille ingredients in a very hot pan. When almost cooked, put on a sheet pan to cool slightly. Add crumbled goat cheese.

For Rosemary Sauce: saute onions in 1 Tbsp butter, add rosemary, cook for one minute. Add white wine, reduce by two-thirds. Add veal stock, reduce by one half. Whisk in remaining 1 Tbsp butter. Strain.

To serve: divide ratatouille into four equal portions and mound on each plate. Pour sauce around ratatouille and serve warm.

Grilled Chicken Breast
with Black Beans & Goat Cheese Sauce

▼▼▼

Serves 2

2 5-oz boned chicken breasts
salt
pepper
1 cup black beans
2 cups chicken stock
1 bay leaf
1 branch of thyme
⅓ of a carrot
⅓ of an onion

⅓ branch celery
2 cloves
1 pinch of salt
12 oz of white wine
3 chopped shallots
6 oz heavy cream
3 oz goat cheese
dash of white pepper
1 Tbsp butter

Sauce:
12 oz white wine
3 shallots, chopped
6 oz heavy cream
3 oz goat cheese
dash of white pepper
1 Tbsp butter

To prepare: soak the black beans 6 to 8 hours prior to cooking. Combine soaked beans, stock, bay leaf, thyme, celery, cloves, onion and salt in a pot and bring to a boil; skim all impurities. Cook until beans are semi-soft (about 1½ hours).

Grill the chicken breasts with salt and pepper. Slice the chicken, put it on a plate and add the black beans on the side, and top the chicken with the sauce.

For sauce, reduce white wine and shallots by half. Add cream and reduce by half. Put in a blender, add goat cheese, butter, then strain, season and reheat over low heat.

RAINIER.
The Only Beer.

3100 Airport Way South
Seattle, Washington 98134
(206) 622-2600

Beer is a satisfying, cooling beverage and because of that many people forget it is also a great seasoning agent. Beer can turn the most ordinary foods into exceptional party fare, adding a surprising subtle quality to many dishes.

Substitute beer for water while simmering meat, or use it as a tantalizing marinade for seafood, fish or meats. In roasting, baking or broiling, beer is used to baste the foods or as an ingredient in the basting sauce to impart a rich, dark color and highlight the gravy. The alcohol evaporates during cooking leaving behind delicate, intriguing flavors.

Used in baking, beer adds a lightness and buoyancy to biscuits, pancakes, cakes, and breads. Experiment with beer as all or part of the liquid in package mixes to reconstitute instant or freeze-dried foods.

Rainier Brewing Company offers free tours Monday–Friday, 1:00–6:00 PM. Come see us!

'R' Barbecue Sauce

Makes 2 cups

½ cup molasses or brown sugar
¼ cup prepared mustard
½ cup catsup
1 tsp Worcestershire

½ cup finely chopped onion
½ tsp salt
¼ tsp black pepper
½ cup Rainier Beer

Combine all ingredients in saucepan; bring to boil. Simmer 5 minutes.

Use generously to baste hamburgers while broiling.

Hot Spiced Ale

▼▼▼

Makes about 3 quarts

12 small apples
¼ cup brown sugar
1 cup sugar
1 tsp cinnamon
1 tsp ginger

1 tsp nutmeg
1½ cups orange juice
1½ cups cranberry juice
2 quarts Rainier Ale

Peel, core and bake the apples in a 350° oven for 30 minutes with a little water and the brown sugar.

While that's going, mix one cup of sugar with the cinnamon, ginger and nutmeg in a large pot. Add the orange juice and cranberry juice. Add the Rainier Ale. Heat, but do not boil, for 15 minutes. Float apples in the hot spiced brew.

Chocolate Layer Cake

▼▼

Makes 1 cake

2 squares (ounces) unsweetened
  chocolate
1⅔ cups sifted flour
¼ tsp salt
1½ tsp baking powder

¼ tsp baking soda
½ cup shortening
1 cup sugar
2 eggs
¾ cup Rainier Beer

Preheat oven to 350°. Grease two 8" layer cake pans and dust lightly with flour. Melt the chocolate over hot water. Cool. Sift together the flour, salt, baking powder and soda.

Cream the shortening, gradually adding the sugar; beat until light and fluffy. Add 1 egg at a time, beating well after addition. Stir in chocolate. Add the flour mixture alternately with the beer, mixing until well blended. Turn into cake pans. Bake 25 minutes, or until a cake tester comes out clean. Cool for 5 minutes in the pans and then turn out onto a cake rack. Let cool completely before frosting. Put layers together with whipped cream or butter frosting.

KING 1090
NEWS/TALK RADIO

Official "Bite of Seattle" Radio Station

———————Classic———————
KING FM 98.1

Jim Althoff's **Pasta with Garlic**

▼▼▼

Serves 4

3 Tbsp butter

3 Tbsp olive oil

3-4 cloves garlic

pasta, fresh or dried

pinch basil

pinch marjoram

pepper

salt

parmesan or romano cheese, grated

1 lb spaghetti

This is a simple and delicious side dish, great with almost any broiled meat or poultry dish.

In a saucepan, heat the butter and olive oil. Peel three or four cloves of fresh garlic and flatten with the wide of a cleaver, the heel of your shoe or whatever else is handy! Add the garlic to the pan, heat slowly over medium-low heat until the garlic begins to turn a bit brown.

Cook the pasta *al dente*. Drain the pasta, toss thoroughly with the garlic-oil-butter mixture. Add a tiny pinch of basil or marjoram, freshly ground pepper and salt to taste. Sprinkle with grated parmesan or romano cheese.

Simple, cheap (so use quality ingredients), foolproof and versatile.

Jim Althoff is KING 1090's talk show host from 9:00 a.m. to noon.

Lisa Brooks' **Miracle**
Microwave Macaroni & Cheese

▼▼▼

Serves 2-4

1 12-oz package elbow macaroni, cooked al dente and drained

8 oz sharp cheddar cheese, grated

⅓ cup grated parmesan cheese

1 4-oz thick slice of smoked ham or turkey, finely grated on a cheese grater

9 saltine crackers, crushed

dried chopped onion

garlic salt

pepper

milk, whole or skim

butter or margarine

Finely coat the bottom of a 9" square micro-safe baking pan with about a third of the crushed crackers, and moisten with 2 Tbsp of milk. Cover with a third of the macaroni, about 3 oz of the cheddar cheese, 1 oz of parmesan and layer with a third of the grated smoked meat. Shake on some of the onions, garlic salt and pepper to taste.

Repeat the layering process (except for the crackers and milk) for two layers, until macaroni is gone. Top the final layer with remaining cracker crumbs, and dab on about a Tbsp of the butter or margarine.

Cook in microwave oven on *high* for 12 minutes, turning once halfway through the cooking cycle. Allow to sit for about 15 minutes before serving.

Lisa Brooks is news anchor on KING 1090.

179

Bryan Lowe's Alexander's Feast

▼▼

Serves 3–4

½ onion, preferably red, diced

½ package frozen okra, sliced

½ lb imitation crab

1 cup of cottage cheese

3 stalks of celery, sliced

2 tsp curry powder

½ cup almonds, chopped

½ tart apple, cut into small pieces

Decide how you wish to present this dish. It is excellent stuffed into precooked manicotti tubes and covered with a sauce of yogurt and curry powder. Then bake for about 20 minutes in a 375° oven in a covered dish. A more traditional treatment would have this dish mixed with an exotic white rice. You should feel free to add anything you have left over in the refrigerator. I have added asparagus or cashews or....

Saute chopped onion in a dab of butter until lightly browned. Add sliced okra and saute until it just begins to brown. Add crab and saute for another few minutes, then add cottage cheese; saute until it starts to melt. Add curry powder and sliced celery and saute for another few minutes. Add a few grinds of fresh pepper.

At the last minute, add diced apples and nuts. Serve with chutney.

Bryan Lowe is heard 5:30 a.m. to 10:00 a.m. on KING FM's Morning Drive.

Jean Enersen's "Fast & Beautiful" Meal

▼▼

Serves 2

2 cups chicken chunks, cooked	*Dessert:*
¾ cups mayonnaise	½ orange
1 cup nuts	sherbet
1 cup green grapes	mint
2 Tbsp curry powder	chocolate syrup

Mix ingredients for chicken salad (first column) and chill. You can put this mixture inside ½ a canteloupe and add a pansy or a rose to the top as garnish.

For the dessert: fill ½ an orange (fruit scooped out) with sherbet and freeze. It's ready in the freezer whenever company drops in. Add a sprig of mint and drizzle chocolate syrup over the top.

Jean Enersen anchors "KING 5 News with Jean Enersen" and co-anchors "KING 5 News: The 6:00 Report."

Rich Marriott's **Chicken Kiev**

▼▼

Serves 4-6

½ tsp garlic flakes

1 tsp basil

1 tsp oregano

dash of salt

3-4 slices of sourdough or other bread

½ cup soft margarine

6-8 chicken breast halves, boned & skinned

¼ cup vermouth

¼ cup green onions, sliced

Preheat oven to 375°.

Mix the garlic flakes, basil, oregano, and salt with the bread slices in a food processor. (Or you can use commercial bread crumbs and mix in a bowl, but this usually will add calories and fats.)

Melt ¼ cup margarine. Dip the chicken breasts in the melted margarine and coat with bread crumb mixture and place in a shallow baking pan. Bake in the oven for about 50-60 minutes or until dark golden brown.

While it's baking, melt the other ¼ cup margarine and mix in the onions and the vermouth.

Pour the sauce over the chicken and cook for another 5 minutes.

Rich Marriott is the weather forecaster for the weekend editions of "KING 5 News." He says about this recipe: "If you suffer from cholesterol problems, this is a safe meal, adapted with few changes from the low fat recipes in the book *Eater's Choice*. It is a great tasting recipe and it is low in calories, cholesterol and saturated fats. And, even though it's healthy, it's a favorite with our kids. If you react poorly to onions or garlic, you can leave these out without hurting the taste of the final dish."

Lori Matsukawa's **Tiny Meat Loaf**

▼▼▼

Serves 4

1 lb ground turkey or beef

1 egg

½ cup dry bread crumbs

⅓ cup catsup

1 Tbsp milk or water

1 envelope (¼ oz) instant soup

This is a recipe for busy families – a microwave version of a tasty meatloaf.

Combine all ingredients and shape into a loaf. Put in shallow microwave dish. Cover with wax paper.

Microwave medium-high for about 16 minutes.

Lori Matsukawa is co-anchor of "KING 5 Morning News," and co-host of "Celebrate the Differences."

Susan Michaels' **Vegetarian Stuffed Peppers**

▼▼

Serves 4

4 green or red sweet peppers, tops
   and seeds removed

1 cup each: chopped onions,
   broccoli, carrots, mushrooms

2 cups cracked bulgur wheat

2 cups vegetable bouillon

¼ tsp dill

¼ tsp oregano

½ tsp salt

Steam peppers for about 5 minutes and remove from stove. Bring bouillon to boil in a large saucepan, add bulgur and stir. Add vegetables and spices. Simmer until moisture is absorbed, about 15 minutes.

Fill peppers with above mixture and cover with favorite tomato sauce. Bake at 350° for 20 minutes.

Variations: add chopped nuts to bulgur mixture. Or use in stuffed cabbage or for "meat" balls or "meat" loaf.

Susan Michaels is co-host of "Seattle Today." She says about this recipe: "The stuffing for the peppers is one I love because it offers a unique, 'nutty' texture. This dish is all vegetarian, yet makes a *complete* protein and balanced meal because of the combination of grains and vegetables. It's very tasty, filling and yet low in calories, cholesterol and fat."

Larry Schick's Cool Summer Bean Burros

▼▼

Serves 2-4

1 package taco seasoning mix
½ cup oil
3 Tbsp white vinegar
½ Tbsp sugar
1 can (16 oz) drained kidney
   beans

¼ cup sliced olives
½ cup chopped tomatoes
peppers (optional)
flour tortillas
1 cup Monterey Jack cheese,
   shredded

A great recipe for a cool, quick, easy summer meal that does not involve cooking.

Mix together all ingredients. Place mixture on flour tortillas and sprinkle shredded Monterey Jack cheese on top. Wrap tortillas around filling.

You can make a big batch of the mixture to put in bowls for camping, picnics, etc.

Larry Schick is the "KING 5 Morning News" weather forecaster.

from the Kitchens
_of_
I.P.I. Publishing

Jood's Famous

Chicken & Vegetable Special

▼▼▼

Serves 2–4

4 boneless chicken breasts, diced

3 medium red potatoes, cubed

2 carrots, sliced

½ medium stalk of broccoli, cut into florets

12-16 Brussels sprouts

1 medium onion, diced

1-2 cloves of garlic, minced

salt, pepper, parmesan cheese

2 Tbsp vegetable oil

Saute diced chicken, garlic and onion in 2 Tbsp vegetable oil until lightly brown. Put in large bowl and keep warm in oven (200°).

Steam remaining vegetables until done. Combine chicken and vegetables. Season with salt and pepper to taste. Heat through and sprinkle with fresh parmesan. That's it – you're done!

Clams & Sausage with Pasta

▼▼▼

Serves 2–4

4 mild/sweet Italian sausage

1 lg red bell pepper

1 lg onion

3-4 cloves garlic

2 tsp olive oil

⅓ cup full bodied red wine

5-6 ripe Italian plum tomatoes, coarsely chopped

2 dozen fresh steamer clams

3 handfulls penne, mostacioli, or other tubular pasta

1 + handfulls bow-tie pasta

freshly grated parmesan or romano cheese

½ tsp dried red pepper flakes

⅓ cup water or white wine

Place sausages in large fry pan and cover with water. Cover pan and bring to boil. Reduce heat and cook ten minutes. Drain water from pan. Prick sausages to let fat drain. Remove sausages to paper towels until cool enough to handle and slice in ¼" rounds.

Slice red pepper into ⅛" wide vertical strips and then halve crosswise. Halve onion and slice thinly. Thinly slice garlic.

Heat 1 Tbsp of olive oil in pan with sausage drippings until very hot. Add peppers, onions and garlic and dry until onions begin to brown, stirring frequently to prevent burining, about 8-10 minutes.

Add sausage rounds and reduce heat to medium; continue frying until sausage is browned. Cook over low heat 20-25 minutes. Add chopped tomato and continue cooking until tomatoes are soft and sausage mixture is thick.

While sausage and onions cook, steam clams in ⅓ cup water or wine until shells open. Remove clams from shells; add to sausage and tomatoes. Add red pepper flakes and stir all together.

continued on the following page.

189

Place remaining Tbsp olive oil and a little minced garlic in large serving dish and place in warm oven.

Bring large pot of water to boil for pasta. Cook until tender and drain. Remove serving dish from oven. Add pasta and toss with oil and a little cheese.

Place sausage and clams in separate bowl. Pass pasta and clam sauce separately and let each diner top pasta with sauce and fresh parmesan.

Makes 2-plus main course servings or 4 first course servings.

❉ T·R·E·S B·O·N ❉
A Unique Collection of Housewares

From C'est Moo Pie to Veal Marsala, you'll find housewares for your every creation.

Our housewares department has everything you need to prepare an endless variety of dishes. Our recipe for success: incomparable selection and quality, plus a knowledgeable staff ready to help. We offer the best names in housewares, too, such as Calphalon, Henckels, Krups, Cuisinart and more. Whether you're searching for the perfect skillet or espresso maker, the sharpest knife or the quickest grinder, The Bon Marche is the main ingredient for equipping your kitchen.

THE BON MARCHÉ

I.P.I. Publishing
10245 Main Street, Suite 8-3
Bellevue, Washington 98004
(206) 454-8473

Please send me _____ copies of **The Bite of Seattle Cookbook** at $12.95 each (plus $1.04 sales tax [Wash. residents] and $2.00 postage and handling: Total $15.99)

Also available: **A Gulp of the Rain City** – alcoholic & non-alcoholic specialty drinks. Please send me _____ copies of **A Gulp of the Rain City** at $4.95 each (plus $.40 sales tax [Wash. residents] and $2.00 postage and handling: Total $7.35)

Enclosed is my check for $_____.

Name_____

Address_____

City_____State_____Zip_____

☐ This is a gift. Send directly to:

Name_____

Address_____

City_____State_____Zip_____

- (Cut Here) --

I.P.I. Publishing
10245 Main Street, Suite 8-3
Bellevue, Washington 98004
(206) 454-8473

Please send me _____ copies of **The Bite of Seattle Cookbook** at $12.95 each (plus $1.04 sales tax [Wash. residents] and $2.00 postage and handling: Total $15.99)

Also available: **A Gulp of the Rain City** – alcoholic & non-alcoholic specialty drinks. Please send me _____ copies of **A Gulp of the Rain City** at $4.95 each (plus $.40 sales tax [Wash. residents] and $2.00 postage and handling: Total $7.35)

Enclosed is my check for $_____.

Name_____

Address_____

City_____State_____Zip_____

☐ This is a gift. Send directly to:

Name_____

Address_____

City_____State_____Zip_____

Kitchen Notes:

Kitchen Notes:

Kitchen Notes: